TIME NO LONGER

——

TIME NO LONGER

AMERICANS
AFTER
THE AMERICAN
CENTURY

PATRICK SMITH

Yale

UNIVERSITY PRESS

New Haven & London

Yale University Press books may be purchased in quantity for educational,
business, or promotional use. For information, please e-mail sales.press@
yale.edu (U.S. office) or sales@yaleup.co.uk (U.K. office).

Designed by Lindsey Voskowsky.
Set in Adobe Caslon Pro and Whitney types by Newgen North America.
Printed in the United States of America.

Library of Congress Cataloging-in-Publication Data

Smith, Patrick (Patrick L.)
Time no longer : Americans after the American century / Patrick Smith.
pages cm
Includes bibliographical references and index.
ISBN 978-0-300-17656-8 (cloth : alk. paper) 1. United States—
Civilization—21st century. 2. National characteristics, American.
3. United States—Historiography—Social aspects. 4. United States—
History—20th century—Historiography. 5. Spanish-American War,
1898—Historiography. 6. Cold War—Historiography. 7. War on
Terrorism, 2001–2009—Historiography. I. Title.
E169.12.S6117 2013
973.93—dc23
2012044389

A catalogue record for this book is available from the British Library.

This paper meets the requirements of ANSI/NISO Z39.48-1992
(Permanence of Paper).

10 9 8 7 6 5 4 3 2 1

This book is for Sara Vagliano,
affection and high regard.

It is for Lloyd Garrison,
traveler on trying trails.

The world is a great dodger, and the Americans the greatest. Because they dodge their very selves.

—D. H. Lawrence,
Studies in Classic American Literature, 1923

CONTENTS

INTRODUCTION

Between Myth and History

Americans, by a long tradition, have been enduringly enamored of stories—tales as to whence they came and who had come before them. This is hardly a unique trait: All people have stories (of one kind or another), stories that tell them (one way or another) something about who they are.

The Greeks had stories, famously enough, and etched them into the stars. The English had many grand stories once, too—stories of great civilizational accomplishment. But the ancient Greeks are gone, and the English, with history at their backs as if it were the wind, have overcome their love of stories. They do not, we can at least say, any longer live by them. They do not make use of stories to determine what they should do or what their place in the world should be. To put the point another way, the English live in history now—humanly determined, humanly made history.

America's stories have come to be many—old ones elaborated and new ones told by each generation. So there is the story of America's stories now. These stories are rooted in the nation's foundational myths. Not everyone considered American, one must quickly add, accepts these myths or any of the stories that arise from them. Critiquing them or rejecting them or simply not knowing them is also understood now to be part of the American story. Nonetheless, America's myths and stories have always possessed an unusual, possibly unique power. Stories differ from history in that they necessitate belief. America's stories, inspiring a deep and extended belief, have driven America on since long before—a century and a half before—America had even declared itself a nation. And they were as affecting, as motivating, and as defining of America and what it did during what we now call the American century as they were amid the late-medieval remains of seventeenth-century Europe.

———

Ours is a singular moment, for the American century is behind us now. This is the starting point of the essays that follow, and it bears many implications, some of which are already becoming evident. America's wars in Afghanistan and Iraq, for instance: It is possible now to speculate, at least tentatively, that these will be the last wars America wages in the name of the mission it assumed by way of its traditional idea of itself. But lying beneath any such practical matter or policy or decision in one or another place around the planet, something else requires our attention now: The power of America's stories and myths is receding like a once-incessant tide along a vast beach. Try as some or many of us may to keep them alive, stories and myths can drive the nation forward no longer and no farther. Americans can no longer pretend to live within them and be part of them or add to them, to make the point another way. Or yet another: It is America that must now learn to live in history—humanly made history and all the attendant "terrors of time," as Mircea Eliade, a prominent writer on myths and history, put it on many occasions.

These essays begin with the thought that our moment is comparable in magnitude to that proclaimed by the larger-than-life millenarians who put America on its course nearly four centuries ago. The vision that John Winthrop did much to shape and set in motion in his "City upon a Hill" sermon in 1630 is now an exhausted narrative. There is no such place and never has been. To recognize this will be, for many Americans, a great dis-illusioning. This is a positive prospect. It will bring difficulties, surely, and it will take time. But it will change Americans in ways they urgently need to change.

One cannot ask to live in (or be excused from) times any more interesting. The pieces that follow are not, nonetheless, another of America's numerous jeremiads—or, to take the fashionable term for the same thing, another shard of declinist prediction. And it should be plain enough already that neither are they an effort to re-enchant Americans with an idea of themselves that, in any case, many have been uncertain of during most of the American century itself. These essays concern a nation that has many choices to make. These choices will be formidable, but we can take the having of them to be a salutary position in which to find ourselves.

How to live, how Americans might understand themselves (among themselves and among others), how to act and advance in a new, yes, post–American century: All of this must be determined to accommodate a new era. Until now, America's myths and stories did this work. The mission was set, all dissent sooner or later absorbed into it, and the task was not to change in any new circumstance but to carry on as before. An elaborate collection of national stories has preserved the notion that America enjoyed an exemption from time itself. It is in this way that America now finds itself suspended between myth and history—the one failing us at last, the other with a beckoning finger raised.

No more succinct description of the American condition seems possible as I begin these pieces. Prevalent habits of mind have rendered America, if not all who dwell in it, not quite capable of discerning the features of a new century and not quite capable, either, of changing to accommodate the turning of history's wheel. As a nation, America cannot yet imagine a future for itself at a moment that demands this imagining because it enjoys no true understanding of where it has been—how it arrived at its present moment. Nietzsche made this connection in the 1870s in his well-known essay about "the uses of history for life," and many others have made the point since. Without the past, one lives "unhistorically," as the German thinker put it, "in blissful blindness between the hedges of past and future."[1]

Blissful Americans do not now seem to be. But how so many of them came into a certain condition of blindness, the price Americans (and many others) have paid for this, and what Americans now, no longer in the seventeenth or eighteenth century but coming to themselves in the twenty-first, can do to remedy their predicament—these are the subjects of the essays that follow.

———

I began to consider these four pieces in the mid-1990s, having not long earlier concluded a lengthy sojourn abroad. That time away had given me something I had not anticipated, something akin to what the historian C. Vann Woodward, in another context entirely, once called a combination of detachment and sympathy.[2] In conversation I sometimes described it as a second pair of eyes. Learning from others had been my work: I had served many years as a correspondent overseas. Then, quite gradually, I began to discover how much I had also learned of myself and my country and the people who lived in it. The experience I describe is nothing unique: It is common enough among expatriates. It derives simply from distance and perspective, and I have asserted the value of acquiring these ways of seeing in other things I have written.

These pieces changed shape more or less continuously as the 1990s went on. How could they not during the decade of that twilight-zone triumphalism in which many Americans indulged at the Cold War's end? I let them change: titles, themes, organization, what had to go in, what could be left unsaid, what time had made obvious or had refuted. The one constant dimension of the essays was the dysfunctional relationship it seemed to me too many Americans had with their own past—to say nothing of anyone else's. This did not change. No matter what I read or thought or saw or talked of with others, I could not push this national neurosis, as it came to seem, off the table. It seemed the root of so much that was coming, ever more evidently in those years, between Americans and Americans and between Americans and the rest of the world.

In the autumn of 2001 all changed utterly, to borrow Yeats's famous line. It was not a terrible beauty that arrived but a terrible clarity, so blinding in the raw truth of it that many Americans—most, perhaps—flinched from it. I was invited then to write an interpretive work about the meaning of September 11; I have never regretted declining and never envied those who went ahead with such projects. That season marked the end of something—but it was something very large, something that would require time to understand, and nothing could substitute for this needed time. Those alive and watching that day were brought face to face with the way momentous events occur in the same quotidian chronology as anything else. As I read it then and as I note in the last of these pieces, the American century ended on an otherwise fine, sunny, Indian summer morning. We remember it as we remember what we were doing and where we were the moment President Kennedy was assassinated. And what we recall, safe to say, is astonishing to most of us for being so unexceptional, so ordinary in proximity to so extraordinary an event. Most of us have done those ordinary things many times since that morning, but for none has it been the same.

These essays take their shape, then, primarily from the century Henry Luce famously named midway through it. The last three of them happen to have as their starting points the beginning, the high point in the middle, and the end of Luce's creative notion. But they do not offer a history: That has been accomplished by scholars abler than I in the professional historian's art and craft. These four pieces are attempts to discover features of the 103-year period called the American century that seem important to grasp if Americans are to understand themselves and where they are now in the human story. What is it that remains? What is it Americans can salvage and what discard? Few of us seem to fathom even the questions, to say nothing of seeking their answers.

To inquire in this way as to the American condition, now that we have begun our second decade after the century named for us, is somewhat like walking among the shells on a beach after the tide has gone out. The sand is firm, but there is a give to it under one's feet. With each step it is remolded and takes a new shape. Some shells lying in it are intact; in some there is beauty, and some others have been cracked by time and the rolling sea and can be abandoned, as the creatures that once lived in them have already done.

———

The first of these pieces, "History Without Memory," is intended primarily as historical background for those that follow. Hence it is the briefest of the four. It concerns the contradiction I find between a profound love of history among many Americans and the nation's place among the great forgetters of the human community. How can this be? My answer is that we have too easily satisfied ourselves, from the very beginning of America as an idea, with the condition named in the essay's title—this is to say a substitution of myth and story for authentic history, things genuinely remembered. If the thought of "national character" were valid (and I do not think it is), this would have to feature among America's traits. A people given to emotional judgments and occasional fevers, Americans have from the start been trained to accept simplistic myths as truths. In consequence, too many of us are lovers of "history," with quotation marks, but take little notice of history.

The second of these essays, "A Culture of Representation," concerns the climate, the atmosphere, the reigning frame of mind—I do not know quite what it is best called—that prevailed at the start of the American century. This I take to have been in the spring of 1898, when Theodore Roosevelt dispatched Commodore Dewey from Hong Kong to the Philippines, promptly resigned his post at the Department of the Navy, and then helped lead the American invasion of Spanish-held Cuba. This is typically understood to be America's bursting-at-the-seams leap onto "the world stage," as it is inevitably called, and it was that. But when scrutinized, the moment was more complex than we customarily understand. What lay beneath the surface in the restless nation eager to make its mark? Look closely and we find a mix of things, some of them unlikely in combination.

TR declared the American century open, Frederick Jackson Turner having codified it five years earlier, and Woodrow Wilson would make a coherent-sounding policy—a benign, utopian internationalism at first—to explain it such that it could be advanced in councils of state. But why all of this? What were Americans think-ing, or—better put, surely—what feeling? For feeling American had always been primary to the condition of being American. To under-stand this would be to recognize some of the fundamental drives that still urge America on—and some that hold America out of the twenty-first century.

Two decades after Germans dismantled the Berlin Wall and the Soviet Union collapsed, many Americans, and perhaps most, seem at least that much time from an understanding of the immense, transformative influence of the Cold War years. This mutation (as I consider it) was one primarily of consciousness, and it is the subject of the third of these pieces, "Cold War Man," a phrase I borrow with gratitude from the scholar Philip Mirowski. It seemed well suited to my purpose when I first came across it in Mirowski's extraordinary book *Machine Dreams*. The Cold War had made Americans some-thing approximating a new species, albeit one with ancestors. This I had long sensed, if unconsciously, having lived through the period more or less in its entirety. Mirowski's phrase provided a dispensa-tion to explore the thought, and this is my intent in the second essay.

April and August of 1945 found America in a position we, look-ing back, might consider truly unprecedented. It had the world's strongest navy and air force and one of the two strongest armies. It had (by itself for four years) an atomic bomb. The war had been just and had shown America, at least in the popular imagination and stripped of certain large events, at its best. With all this in view, what ensued seems all the more extraordinary now that the Cold War is over (if not yet truly behind us).

It was during the Cold War years that the myths by which Amer-ica had long lived its national life reached their most compelling and propelling phase. They lay behind nearly everything Americans did, and so became the one way America could explain what course it would follow from 1947 onward. Unconscious drives seemed to take over the nation's leaders and many of its led. Paranoia and anxiety, latent among Americans since the eighteenth century but the last things one would expect to see evinced in the decisive victor of a war of World War II's magnitude, became for many the ruling compulsions. Wilsonian idealism—the ambition to bear democracy abroad as if it were a torch in the darkness—became something else, a monstrous and costly betrayal of itself and of others. Neo-Wilsonian idealism was the very most indulgent name for it.

And in combination with the dominance of the unconscious came a hyperrationality that between them produced the very oddest of belief structures—one based on nostalgia and science, a looking back and a peering forward all at once. Both took on the attributes of a faith. It is a faith in which many Americans—though, as from the beginning, by no means all—still believe. Certainly it touches many of us professing not to believe in it, for it gives us more of our numerous stories and it proves persistent. This is the ground created and developed by Cold War man.

"The American of the future will bear but little resemblance to the American of the past."[3] That is Edwin Seligman, a prominent economist of his time, lecturing at Columbia in 1902. He had different matters on his mind then, but Americans can now make use of the observation nonetheless. Seligman's concerns, at bottom, were democracy and empire and how each of these, and Americans, would turn out in a new time; he was a proponent of what scholars call historicity at precisely the moment when the timeless, enduring myths were leading America into its first global adventures. Democracy and empire are America's concerns once more—and so the subjects of the last of these essays, "Time and Time Again." Equally, the Progressive-era thinker seemed to suggest the possibility of change in the manner and prevailing assumptions of American life—that

Americans might engage in the modern act of "becoming." The essay takes this, too, as a starting point.

It would have been less plausible to claim such a beginning as I started to shape these pieces more than a decade and a half ago. A change of any kind, to say nothing of a fundamental change in direction, seemed more or less out of the question then. Why should America change, one may as well have asked, if what it has done all along has turned out so well? It is the logic of any victor one can name in history. But the logic itself changed in 2001, for that September contained the moment when history arrived decisively on American shores, and neither sacred space nor sacred time would ever again provide Americans sanctuary from those terrors I have mentioned earlier.

To turn the triumphant declaration of an eighteenth-century historian on its head, the orthodox idea of America had time no longer after 2001. It had been a question among some thinkers at least since the late Cold War years whether America's founding political heritage was adequate for the time ahead, or whether it had taken the nation as far as it ever would. Suddenly, a combination of many varied factors seemed to announce an answer. As a nation, Americans were face to face with a world no longer hospitable (as it had once seemed to be) to a people propelled by mythological renderings of themselves. At home, the anxiety and doubt long hidden beneath the impulse constantly to assert a supposedly inalienable confidence became less and less deniable—the elephant in the living room. Two and a half centuries of the American story—four if we go back to the beginning—had come to a close. For us the question remains the same: Are we properly equipped for our time? The more pressing matter is whether Americans will prove willing to ask and answer it.

The four essays that make up this book are given to a single purpose, then: to sound the tense strings wound between the pegs of myth and history during the hundred years and a few that I take to be the span of the American century. It is this high, piercing tone that Americans now have a chance to render, hear, and recognize all at once, it seems to me. We have neither sounded it nor heard it yet, and it is this silence that leaves so many Americans so divided and confused—so lost, most important, as to their place in a world that knows all about change and is changing more swiftly than ever in history. When we break this silence, assuming we find the will to do so, we will be in a position to write a composition, if I may risk extending the musical metaphor, and something that suggests not a conclusion but the new music to come.

———

This brief résumé of the essays to follow implies ruptures in American life during the very recent past. I count two, possibly three: one as the American century commenced, one at its conclusion, and maybe another at its midway mark, if we wish to count the Cold War's onset as such. The first of these, and the second if we count it, opened up the nation to a constructive kind of change—a prospect that America turned out to deflect in each case. Now, with the third rupture in our modern history just behind us, Americans have the same choice once again. And once again many of us are filled with uncertainty, covered now by the thinnest veil of national confidence. Just as Americans were in the 1890s, they are once more divided between those standing in vigorous defense of America's exceptionalism, holding fast to a mythological understanding of the nation's identity and place, and those urging a historical point of view upon us. "It All Ended as It Began" was one title I earlier contemplated for this collection, and I mention it here simply because it makes the point plainly enough.

My summary of what follows may also suggest that Americans must consider the century given their name a failure. True enough, the American era proved, even before it was over and certainly in its final years and its immediate aftermath, nearly the nation's undoing. The time of America's overweening predominance was, in the kind of judgment now needed, a costly and destructive interim—with the exception of the Civil War the worst thing to befall the republic since it was founded a century before the American century began. It was unbecoming of Americans in many of its passages and fated from the first not to last—a point many of us have yet to grasp. "Failure" is too strong and categorical a term for so long and complex a time. "Success," by the same token and from the point of view I urge in these pieces, is out of the question.

It is near to de rigueur these days for any writer producing a narrative of America's present predicament to come to an inspirationally optimistic conclusion. We may dwell in a post-American world, for instance, but America can somehow remain its indispensable leader nonetheless. No one else is equipped for the task, and like it or not we must stay the course—another common line of argument. I rather abhor this feature of the national conversation. It is an argument settled safely within the confines of exceptionalism, and exceptionalism is a national impediment America can no longer afford. Disturbance and discomfort, a jarring loose from one's moorings, are sometimes necessary for the sake of an authentic advance. And America is now more or less urgently in need of such a jarring loose and such an advance.

Neither do I care for a pessimism as to America's future that seems to reign nearly supreme in our private conversation, even as our public discourse—Eastern Europe–like—tilts farther and farther in the opposite direction. Along with many others, I have sometimes been marked down as a declinist, but this label misses the point. The ending of something is the beginning of something else; until the world ends the two are not separable. This is the position articulated in these pages. The end and the beginning open the nation to numerous possibilities.

It is not clear to me whether the deep anxieties any of us can identify in American life now arise from a suspicion that America's time is over or whether the nation is daunted more by the idea of departure, a new start. The difference is important to note, and I suspect that the latter lies at the core of our twenty-first-century neurasthenia. Beginnings require choices, and choices are made by human beings, not the tilting of any providential hand: Choices, in short, are made in history, that zone Americans, at least by tradition, have presumed themselves to have avoided.

The first of these choices already lies before us—has lain before us, indeed, since 2001. It is also America's most difficult, given the nation's background and proclivities. It is the choice of whether we will recognize all the other choices the nation will face. Americans are accustomed to neither choices nor change, insist as they will on their desire for the one and their capacity to manage the other better than anyone else. In my view, and given how quickly the world spins around us, Americans have about twenty-five years to make up their minds on this fundamental point. This is the "time no longer" of our time. Counting from 2001, part of this brief passage has already been spent, and I am hardly the first to consider the opening ten years of our new century as America's lost decade.

"To dissent is to declare one's optimism," a friend once told me of his views of his own country (which happened to be India). "Why would I bother otherwise?" With this thought in mind I confess to a certain optimism—a glint of positive expectation. The only thing that makes America exceptional any longer (if it ever were such) is its persistent claim to exceptionalism. The inspiring aspect of this observation is that America has an opportunity now to step down from the marble pedestal it erected for itself nearly two and a half centuries ago.

"Americans are alone in the world," Luigi Barzini announced in a book he published in 1953. The noted Italian journalist meant this admiringly (as he did everything he wrote about us), but in this, an extraordinary insight, he did not describe a happy condition. A certain aloneness has always been part of what it means to be American—an apartness from others Americans typically profess to prefer—and the American century led us ever deeper into this solitude. This is what Barzini saw at midpoint. But it need not, if we choose otherwise, be the American's fate any longer. And it is in favor of an embrace of this new condition that I have composed these pieces.

———

Can America transform itself from a nation with a destiny into a nation with a purpose? Herbert Croly, the prominent social critic of the Progressive era, posed this question a century ago, just after the first of the ruptures I have mentioned. It had been ten years since America had launched itself into the world beyond its shores bearing the banner of "manifest destiny." And Croly's distinction was essential then to grasp: Purpose pushes people into the stream of history, where authentic decisions must be made on the basis of "what is"—a favored phrase among thinkers and scholars in Croly's time. Destiny holds people out of history, in the space of timeless mythologies, where there are no choices or decisions. Purpose gives a nation tasks, challenges, things to think about and attend to, while destiny leads merely to semisacred "missions," abstractly conceived undertakings people can scarcely explain even to themselves.

A little more than a century after Croly published *The Promise of American Life*, his question is precisely ours. America is to become a nation like others, those unique aspects of its past notwithstanding. This is not anyone's choice: It is history turning forward. The primary choice lies in whether Americans do this creatively, with imagination and some measure of inspiration—an embrace of fate, a perspective on things as they are—or with reluctance, a certain denial, that condition of blindness already evident among us. The former alternative holds out the promise Croly longed for (and never saw fulfilled) a century back, a certain reconceived idea of greatness that does not now seem to many of us either great or within reach. But do this, and America might truly break history's mold. Others have accomplished it, not least the Spanish (and at our insistence). A century ago they took what appeared to the naked eye to be a drastic loss and made of it, in our time, long years later, a gain—an outgrowing of an idea of themselves that had become burdensome and no longer of any use.

HISTORY WITHOUT MEMORY

—

What nation knows so little of its own beginnings?
—Waldo Frank, *The Re-Discovery of America*, 1929

Myths are more or less universal to humankind. Although we often assume that societies leave myths behind as they advance, this is not necessarily so. The postulation is that an empirical or scientific consciousness pushes the mythical consciousness into the past. But there is no such equation. In some nations we may find this—the premodern giving way cleanly to the modern. But others, counter-intuitively, do the reverse: Japan became an extravagant maker of myths as it modernized in the nineteenth century. Still others simply cling to their myths, and neither science nor empirical thought has anything to do with it. America is the last kind of nation. It has held fast to its myths. This is among the remarkable things about the

American story: So much that was premodern in it has been carried into the modern age.

By the simplest and best definitions, myths are stories that are told and take place outside of time. They contend, then, with historical time and with history itself. Some myths are rooted in repetition. The Greeks, for instance: In their myths we find the archaic notion of circular time. What happened once will happen again, and this return to *illud tempus*, sacred time, is the object of a society's expectations. The availability of a better time that came before is a source of certainty. Other myths are suspended in linear time, and here we can turn to the Jews and their tradition. The prophets proposed to write of events that occurred in the past or the present. But they were understood as divine signifiers and prefigurations of events that were to occur again, in a sacred time to come. This time to come was understood to be the expansion and accomplishment of what had come before and what had been prophesied. So the question of time—its repetition, its beginning again, humankind's escape from it, its eschatological end—is an essential feature shared by myths everywhere.

Myths are also acts of the imagination, or of reason applied imaginatively. Henry Nash Smith, who wrote of the American West, called myth "an intellectual construction that fuses concept and emotion into an image." Myths are also "collective representations," Smith noted in his famous *Virgin Land*, "rather than the work of a single mind."[1] Both of these thoughts help advance our understanding. Almost always myths involve ritual, they derive in some measure from the unconscious, and they are one way we humans can invest the things we do with meaning beyond the meaning that lies within the doing of something by itself.

There are other features of myths to be noted. Myths are intended to convey simple truths, so they have little of history's complexity. At the same time they must be counted as historical phenomena, for they can influence events and what people decide to do within those events. Myths change and can be put to new purposes, and a new myth, embodying the old within it, is taken to be no less true than the myth it replaces.

Myths are generally conservative: They are deployed to justify a given state of affairs or to prompt a given course of action, the outcome of which is advanced as certain. They tend to discourage change by the mere claim that they are true and continue to be true. Myths require belief, so there is a "we-and-they" aspect to them: Either one accepts the truth of a myth or one stands outside of those who do. This means that myths create and sustain group and community identities, or even ideologies; they are often invoked when such identities and ideologies may be in doubt. And it is with these things in mind that we should consider American myths and how they became such.

——

"Wee shall find that the God of Israell is among us, when ten of us shall be able to resist a thousand of our enemies, when hee shall make us a prayse of glory, that men shall say of succeeding plantacions: the Lord make it like that of New England: for wee must Consider that wee shall be as a Citty upon a Hill, the eies of all people are uppon us."[2]

John Winthrop's most famous sermon, "A Model of Christian Charity," is commonly taken to be among the great early visions of the American experiment. Cotton Mather made of him a mythical figure when he published his life of Winthrop in 1702, seventy-two years after the English dissenter delivered himself of his thoughts. He was Nehemias, leader of the Jews in their exit from Babylon, in Mather's title: *Nehemias Americanus*, the brief biography is called. In the text he was "the envy of the many but the hope of those who had any hopeful design in hand," and this made him someone else:

> Accordingly, when the noble design of carrying a colony of chosen people into the American wilderness was by some eminent persons undertaken, this eminent person was, by the consent of all, chosen for the Moses who must be the leader of so great an undertaking. And indeed nothing but a Mosaic spirit could have carried him through the temptations to which either his farewell to his own land or his travel in a strange land must needs expose a gentleman of his education.[3]

Winthrop had never been to America when he talked about his City. We do not know precisely where he was when he preached "A Model of Christian Charity," and we are not sure who, exactly, heard him. It is likely that he was aboard the *Arbella*, the ship that carried him to the Massachusetts coast, or in a church in Southampton, his port of embarkation. We are certain, though, that Winthrop had never seen America but in his mind's eye at the moment of his rhetorical flourish.

To understand him, then, we have to recognize that he was speaking as much in reaction to the past as he was in anticipation of the future. He was striking the pose of a prophet. He was suggesting that the fulfillment of the old prophecies was at hand. But he was thinking of Babylon or Egypt, depending upon which of Mather's mythmaking metaphors we settle with, as much as any promised land. He was English, and so would have been his listeners. We are obliged, then, to recognize that the American story in this early iteration was part of a larger story—a history, indeed—and cannot be told by itself. America was new, but it was not only or wholly new.

And before it was anything it was a myth: This was to prove a fateful beginning.

Winthrop professed to having enemies. Who were these enemies? Mather tells us the world Winthrop was leaving behind faced him with temptations. What temptations were these?

The cultural foundations of medieval Europe were in a state of advanced decay by Winthrop's day. The center of the universe was shifting—down from the infinite heavens and into the temporal world of men and women and their deeds and works. Christian symbols and beliefs were coming gradually to be less compelling as guides to a fleeting life that had been presumed to be but a prelude to the eternal. Time came to be measured and soon enough commodified, and tolling church bells gave way to market-square clocks. Place, for the emerging townsmen and merchants, was not as fixed as it had been. What could be seen would be what counted: There came the empirical mind and what would later be called materialism. Francis Bacon had just announced how knowledge could be abstracted and the physical world might truly be known: the scientific method. Money (abstracted value) came ever more to replace barter in tangible goods of like worth. The individual (at bottom another abstract notion) came into being. All this is simply to describe in brief the earliest stirrings of the arriving modern.

But the advent of much that would make the modern era modern by no means represented a clean break with the past. The Renaissance was not the decisive rupture we customarily think of it as being. It was an interim brought about by a concatenation of circumstances (much as the American century was), and it had a beginning, a middle, and an end (again, not unlike the American century). Much of what was crumbling survived and survived, if only in pieces, for medieval culture had given European humanity a symmetry and completeness and a certainty that the modern would never have on offer. Uncertainty and change—those terrors of time and history Mircea Eliade so often wrote about—disinherited many. Most of society, in any case, was in no part touched by science or commerce or, altogether, the advent of humanism. By the Puritans' day, millenarianism had a tradition in Europe dating back centuries.[4]

This was the world that produced the Protestant movements and John Winthrop, soon enough Cotton Mather, and later on Jonathan Edwards. It was the context out of which came "the new world." We might pause with this phrase to consider how it is customarily articulated, for it was a *world* more than it was *new*. It was new for the simple reason that it was not old, it was "virgin," a beginning again for humanity, meaning nothing of the old world was to contaminate it. But it was more palpably a world because it was distant and unknown, it was seen to be empty, and, again, it was virgin. It offered a certain immunity to those who settled it. The act of crossing, to the earliest settlers, was in its meaning of biblical magnitude. The Atlantic was the longed-for sea of the captive Jews. But the new world's break with the old was not so clean and—in history, if not in myth—never could have been.

In Greek, we should remind ourselves, "world" translates as *kosmos*, which also denotes "order." And to this new cosmos, this new order, flowed all the great currents coursing through late medieval Europe. It was material in its preoccupations such that this would later prove a fault. Its political severance from Europe was made sacred a century and a half after Winthrop sailed the Atlantic. But as the Puritans themselves made plain, the new world was in a certain way old. It was settled, in part, by the unprivileged and dispossessed of Europe, devoted readers of the Old Testament. And it was settled, in another part, by those in rebellion against the arrival of time and history and the descent from heaven of humankind's eyes to the mutable world of decay and disruption and of earthbound human events. Lewis Mumford put the point with unsurpassed clarity and grace in *Sticks and Stones*, the first half of his contemplation of American civilization. "In the villages of the New World there flickered up the last dying embers of the medieval order."[5]

———

In the end we can only imagine how the sight of "virgin land"—the Atlantic littoral being the first of numerous American Wests—must have inspired the early European arrivals to millennial visions of a new *world*. But we have the help of explorers, shipmates, settlers, and others who kept records of their journeys. They suggest a way into the hearts and souls of those in sight of the new world for the first time, and they are all stamped with the same two attributes: There was anticipation and there was anxiety. These are simply two sides of the same consciousness, a consciousness of a future as yet uncertain.

"It doth all resemble a stately park," James Rosier, a diarist on a 1605 exploration, noted of the New England coast and the mouths of its rivers:

> Many who had been travelers in sundry countries, and in the most famous rivers, yet affirmed them not comparable to this they now beheld . . . yet it is no detraction from them to be accounted inferior to this, which not only yields all the aforesaid pleasant profits, but also appears infallibly to us free from all imagined inconveniences.[6]

There were the dangers anyone can imagine, of course: treacherous shoals and inhospitable tides, infinite darkness, Native Americans of uncertain intent, in the case of one French priest a portentous meteor. But "God kept us from great and noteworthy perils," as Father Pierre Biard, the French cleric, sanguinely concluded after his journey in 1611 to the coast of Maine.[7]

There is much of this kind of salutary writing in collections of the old accounts. But there is fear and uncertainty, too, and it is essential to note this. An existential angst that God might not be there after all, or that the new world experiment will have displeased him, or that the myths and prophecies may not prove out: This kind of doubt has been as much a part of American thinking as the mythologies and prophecies themselves. America, in short, has never been so certain a nation as it has pretended from the first to be. "A waste of howling wilderness," a settler wrote (in verse) as he looked inward to the impenetrable forests from the coast in 1662:

> Where none inhabited
> But hellish fiends, and brutish men
> That devils worshipped.[8]

It was amid this mixed consciousness, an eager looking forward and an anxious reticence as to what lay ahead, that the foundational myths took root in the new world. And it is remarkable how in keeping they turn out to be with archetypal myths, age-old myths found here and there throughout many civilizations and eras. There are extensive studies of these myths, some of them assigning myth to primitive humanity. The better thought might be the primitive in humanity, for we find some of the same characteristics in the myths by which Americans would understand what America was. It had come to be as a consequence of ritual hostilities—in the American case beginning with the Puritans and their old world enemies. It was a purification, and one occurring at a high place above the corrupt world of the unchosen: Winthrop's hill with a city atop it. There was a journey required, a deliverance, and it offered an exit from evil to those who made it. In the new world, nature was to be read as divine revelation, the laws of nature being the will of the creator made manifest. Figures and events, altogether, had no meaning in themselves but were understood according to prefiguring narratives—typologies, as a prominent historian has termed them.[9] Winthrop was Moses or Nehemias, and America was not a continent already inhabited by non-Europeans: It was the promised land, empty and awaiting the settlement and civilization of the elect.

Providential nation, chosen people, city upon a hill, a new *world* that was a beacon to the rest, humanity's unique exception: These are America's myths as they solidified. But the most important feature of them had to do with time. America was to be nothing if not a declaration of belief in the new idea of progress. This derived from the late eighteenth century—from Condorcet and the Scottish moralists. Progress rested upon the concept of linear time. But we must look closely at how the American experiment was understood by those who inscribed it with mythological meaning before we draw conclusions from this. Progress can be interpreted as a secularized version of history as the millenarians had it. As became clear in the nineteenth century, it was a faith one believed in.[10] Crossing the Atlantic was a great going forward—the act of modern men. But for those among them of archaic mind, the crossing was also a great going back—back to a land long promised by the prophets. It was an escape from the evils of Europe but also an escape from history's temporal frights. In this respect America represented a regeneration, a renewal by way of a return, and these were understood to occur periodically in the history of humanity.

The profuse biblical imagery of early America makes this plain: Profane time, in which all is subject to decay and the toll taken by history, was left behind for a reentry into sacred time—the *illud tempus* of Eliade's books. The new world offered, more than anything else, an escape from history by way of a millennial return to a world without change. Yes, time was linear, but history was made merely of the details of the larger conception of fallen man on his way to re-demption. It was narrative and metanarrative. "Historical facts thus become 'situations' of man in respect to God," Eliade wrote in *The Myth of the Eternal Return*, "and as such they acquire a religious value that nothing had previously been able to confer upon them."[11]

The point is essential, for this turned out to be among America's most distinguishing features: Europe was where history took place; America was immune from history's ravages. It was changeless. It would measure by way of space the progress it represented—space as an exit from profane time. This was what made the new world truly another world, the distinguishing mark of America's consciousness of itself as an exception: Its land exempted it, most of all and then as now, from the laws of history. To move ever westward was there-fore to escape from historical time into providential time. And in America the available space westward seemed limitless, such that the escape from history could be presumed to be eternal. God would indeed keep Americans from great and noteworthy perils, and hell-ish fiends encountered along the way would be one of two kinds: From behind would come intruders from the historical time Ameri-cans had fled; ahead lay those in need of civilizing by way of the providential word.

The questions of time and change are of fundamental impor-tance to Americans now if they are to understand themselves in the twenty-first century. So is the pervasive self-doubt noted earlier: With a worldly mission as large as America's, true certainty could never be possible. The structure of thinking I have tried briefly to describe has always been tarnished by this apprehension, this fear-inducing doubt. But the metanarrative remains an animating ele-ment in the way many Americans comprehend their relationships: to the past, to the future, and to others. The mythical notions of a land beyond history's borders and a land forever young and never to be in need of change—such things may seem exotic, plucked from another age, but these are the nation's inheritance, the things bequeathed by the early Protestant millenarians. In some Americans, including some American presidents, these things have come down to the present remarkably intact, impervious to all question or challenge. But as I have already suggested, we have come now to a new moment, a reentry into time from whence history and change can no longer be held at bay.

———

Americans, like many others, understand their past as if it lies behind them in discrete layers, like a geological formation. The past of the Puritans and their theocratic states is a deep past for Americans living now, lost to many of us but in the faintest outline. We think little of how this past survives within and among us. And if anything, this process of losing the past is accelerating at a startling rate. At this point, the American past begins, most Americans consider, with the late eighteenth century and the revolution and the founding of the republic. It is there, at least, that the focus sharpens. We have popular biographies galore, numerous each season, of Washington or Jefferson or Adams—political men. Less candescently lit are the eras and religious sentiments of a Winthrop or a Mather or a Jonathan Edwards.

For those alive during the revolution, of course, the time of the Puritans was the immediate past, the first and only layer. The Puritans were their founding fathers, already draped in mythology, just as the revolutionaries are the founding fathers for those living and remembering today. What, then, did the revolutionary period bear forward from its past? What was it that the sons of the fathers, as a historian has evocatively described the revolutionary generation, took with them from their founding fathers? And what was it they added that was new?[12]

Borne forward, good historians tell us, was the idea of the revolution as the fulfillment of the previous century's millenarian expectations.[13] The revolution encompassed many ideas and many narratives, but the revolution as the fulfillment of prophecy was markedly one of them, and there is no rhetoric more powerful than the rhetoric of providential patronage. In other words, the revolution became a new myth. Subsumed within it, perfectly identifiable, were the old seventeenth-century myths, but they had been transformed. A foundational myth, a theocratic myth, had become a political myth, if only in part. The new myth was intended for different purposes—to inspire action against the British crown, to urge settlers to join in the making of a new country. It had new references. So did the original founding fathers pass something on, but so also did they give way to the founding fathers we now associate with the beginning of the nation.

Here we must take care, however. Americans must understand this passage of their past as much or more than other passages if they are to understand themselves now. Millennial accountings of things, many of them based on readings of the prophecies found in Revelation, flowed like mountain streams from New England pulpits before, during, and after the Revolution. New England ministers became priests and prophets. As one historian has written, they were closer to the first century in their sensibilities than they were to ours.[14] For them and for those who worshiped with them, the millennial narrative they naturally inherited gave great clarity to matters of good and evil, clearing away all ambiguities. This became a kind of rhetoric for the revolution—and to an extent that remains plain to us today, an enduringly American rhetoric. For some, it suffused events with an amplitude, a largeness in the face of history—again, just as it would in the postrevolutionary period.

But millenarianism did not give the revolution an ideology. To read around in the period is to discover that it was thick in the air, certainly. And New England ministers indeed carried the seventeenth century into the eighteenth. But they were influenced by the revolution at least as much and probably more than they exerted any influence upon it. It is not altogether unlike the relationship between Christian fundamentalism and national politics that we have seen develop over the past several decades. Can we now say America is a purely secular state, without religious tint? Certainly we cannot, not without qualifying ourselves to take account of the abundance of religious speech and gesture in our political discourse.

This brings us to what was new in late-eighteenth-century America, and the point can be put variously. The revolution gave the world a republic, and this, of course, was a secular advance. Republics are made by men. This left the inheritors of America's religious tradition with a task of interpretation. For some the revolution was an act of translation—a vessel in which to take a religious past into the present, the secular world of nations. For others the revolution seems to have been a religious experience in itself—and so not a translation of anything. What can be taken as plain is that the revolution was undertaken out of more than a cold, careful appraisal of immediate circumstances. Many things contended in early American thinking: the premodern and what was then modern, history and an exemption from it, civic thought and the religious, reason and belief. Of unmistakable influence, however, was a conviction as to destiny and providential intent, however this might have been understood. This is typical of political myths. They frequently account for degrees of bravery and self-sacrifice that cannot otherwise be explained.[15]

One way of understanding the complexity of American myth in the late eighteenth century is to note how quickly it read universal meaning into itself. Even before the war began, Americans had declared that they were not to fight simply the English crown and simply for themselves: They would fight all tyranny and for all humanity. This thought was shared by the secularists and the millenarians alike. And it was a fateful enlargement of the cause; whether it was understood religiously or secularly, it had the seed of empire at its core. Equally, the presence of this kind of myth in eighteenth-century thinking puts civic consciousness and the influence of the *philosophes* in another light. Myth is a contaminant; in relation to historical thought it is a corruption. How, then, did these modes of thought and sentiment—myth and rationality—interact? What emerged, quite quickly, is what we now call a civil religion. This is what has come down to us, its two strands intact. This is why we alive today cannot ignore the seventeenth century and its bequest if we are to understand any century since. "A nation with the soul of a church," an English writer could still describe America in the early twentieth century.[16] From the start, the new republic was adapted to contain a millennial concept of time. It was earthly, for it was humanly made. It was "heavenly," for it was ordained by God—God, the "wise and skillfull Manager," God, "the supreme Governor."[17]

We are now able to think of the revolutionary period with much more complexity than was possible during, say, the first century after it. Good modern historians have put the period before us in richer and more nuanced detail, with greater intellectual density and greater psychological depth, stripped of its accreted myths and stories. This is an important, promising advance. Internal conflict, bitterness and enmity, doubt, fear, divided loyalties, propaganda, eschatology, coercion, cruelty, inequitable suffering, wealth, poverty, and self-interest: All these are available to us as parts of the making of the United States, as inevitably they had to have been. It has all been written about. We can now read the constitution knowing there was a subordinate democratic tradition standing opposite the elite tradition that produced it. This antitradition beside the orthodox tradition has been part of the historical tradition for more than a century.

"It is no easy matter to render the union of independent states perfect and entire," an eighteenth-century historian named Mercy Otis Warren wrote, "unless the genius and forms of their respective governments are in some degree similar."[18] But the genius and forms were not so similar before America became the United States. Of all that was coursing through the thirteen highly fractious colonies at the time of their independence, what bound them together such that they could revolt against their sovereign power, the world's supreme empire at the time, seems to have been the colonists' very large idea of what they were doing, whether it derived from references to the past—the biblical past or the brief American past—or from an En-lightenment reading of history. The English sovereign was "the iron rod of tyranny," and he guarded the gates of hell itself in slovenly corruption. Patriots were modern Israelites, or descendants of the elect. Jehovah was on their side, and "the eyes of the whole world are upon us in these critical times."[19] While millennial logic did not directly intrude upon republican thinking and theorizing, it was for many an invocation, for it called upon the perspective of the (first) founding fathers to convey what religious America considered the revolution's most universal meaning to roughly a million settlers. Those original fathers had bequeathed a sacred tale of origins. The revolution was its fulfillment. In certain aspects it was a form of an-cestor worship, though it signified past and future both.

The spoken and printed literature of the revolutionary era is dense with religious references of this kind. There was an aspect of the time that seems to have been self-evidently sacred to many Americans. To capture this precisely would be like trying to breathe eighteenth-century air: We cannot. Questions arise, but they are perhaps to remain with us ever as questions. We know now that severing relations with England was a wrenching experience for many colonists, for instance. There were spiritual and cultural ties, material ties, family ties. So there is, first of all, the question of belief.

The use of propaganda, from the pulpits to the printing shops, was rampant before and during the hostilities with the British crown. We must ask why these incessant invocations of good and evil and destiny. Taken together are they a measure of hidden doubts? The imagery strongly suggests that America was to be understood as a project requiring belief and faith and feeling rather than thought or considered understanding. But how much were colonists in agreement on the matter? We cannot be certain. Roughly half of male American settlers were illiterate, it is now generally understood, and among women the proportion was three-quarters. But this may or may not have made much difference. The savagery with which Loyalists were treated during and after the war suggests that they were seen primarily as nonbelievers, outside the circle of redemption.[20] At the same time, there is much to suggest that the mythical dimensions of the revolution were primarily the manufacture of those most prominent in the New England clergy—an early use of symbol and imagery to make a system of beliefs and a vision that could be shared. Many heard; we know not how many believed.

A historian writing in the 1970s offers an illuminating passage into another of these questions, the question of the new republic. In his most influential work, *The Machiavellian Moment*, J. G. A. Pocock traces the philosophic root of the American republic to civic humanism as expressed in Renaissance Florence. It then found fertile soil in Britain during the seventeenth century and in America during the eighteenth. In all three places the republic was conceived as the incarnation of an ideal. It was by way of virtuous republican government that humanity arrived at its fullest accomplishment.[21]

This was also part of America's understanding of what it was doing in the late eighteenth century. But the Florentines understood the vulnerability of human creations, for they had inherited a certain idea of time: All that passed from the ideal to the earthly was subject to corruption, decay, and the decline implicit in time's passage. This thought accompanied the republicanism that crossed the Atlantic from England, and it made no contradiction with the thinking of Protestant millenarians: Would the republic stand, the secular expression of the divinely inspired and divinely willed? Or would it be ever fragile in the realm of profane time, ever in need of vigilance and protection if it was to prove a triumph over history? How, in addition, did Americans live with this uncertainty? Progress of the kind the Scottish thinkers favored was an ambiguous proposition: Society might advance by way of markets and commerce, but its virtue might just as easily decay. This is why "progress," as we customarily use the term, was long in gaining acceptance among the revolutionary generation, even as many found it fascinating.

It would be difficult to overstate the prominence of these sentiments in the American inheritance. Amid great confidence, high spirits, and high ideals was the United States born. But it also arose amid an enduring anxiety as to its prospects for survival. This has never left us. American ebullience combined with a certain high-strung tremulousness, a fear of weakness and failure amid feelings of strength: These have ever since coexisted as prevalent features in the uneasy makeup of Americans. The anxious republic made by the founding fathers was a secular creation, but it was born forward in part by way of Protestant millenarian thought. This is a lasting aspect of the American myth as it evolved from religious to secular and political, for the line between the two ways of understanding America was not etched deeply. The fear of internal decay and recidivism, a suspicion of ill-intended others, a hope for the advocacy of Providence: These are part of what Americans mean when they speak of patriotism—or, indeed, "America" as against "the United States." And in combination these habits of mind and sentiment are part of what is supposed to bind Americans together, now as then, and as it was in the beginning.

———

Given that the survival of the republic so quickly became the focus of American anxiety, Americans in the revolutionary period and the years following it erected many defenses against time and the decline it brought with it. America was a political entity, of course, but it would also remain a kind of religious entity. In both cases it still required belief, for even as a worldly republic it was based on a creed. The creation of a nation was nothing if not a historical event, the fullest flower of the Age of Reason. But the Age of Reason, we must always recall, was not altogether a reasonable age. As in early-modern Europe (or anywhere else at any given moment, including ours), the archaic and the arriving new coexisted side by side in early America. It was humanity in its most virtuous state: This is an idea of linear history that could hardly be asserted more unambiguously. But America had also stepped outside of time and history. So did the mythical and religious way of thinking about the United States survive the revolution—and so would it survive well into the next century, primarily by way of Protestant pulpits. America was sacred space, quite distinct now from the profane. The republic served as its earthly frame.

Jefferson had developed another kind of defense against decay, one more rooted in a working idea of history, though it was finally (and fatally) idealist at its core. Long thought to be an atheist but in truth nothing like one, Jefferson was not above invoking the hand of the creator in explaining what he had done so much to bring into being. His beloved American farmers, whom he hoped would make and keep America America, were "the chosen people of God if ever He had a chosen people."[22] From this thought arose Jefferson's vision of a republic kept ever virtuous because it would remain, with land limitless, ever agrarian. Jefferson thus posited virtuous nature and purity against Hamilton's crass and corrupting commerce and the passage of time. Keep crossing the mountain ranges on the way westward, he may as well have said, and he did much during his presidency to encourage this constant tide of settlement.

The fear of time and history lingers, lest this point be taken as a theoretical abstraction or an artifact of an era that is no longer. There is, indeed, a continuity in American ideology and belief that is remarkable when one considers the number of contexts in which it has been applied. For many of us, the fear of history—the fear of existence in a mutable world along with everyone else—remains another part of what it means to be American, and the thought is commonly enough asserted in our own day. The reference to the past, the historical allusion to things already said, is lost, because Americans are so poor at keeping track of their past. So the echoes go unheard. But the point is nonetheless made, just as it might have been two or three centuries ago. "Americans have always made history rather than let history chart our course." That was Henry Kissinger speaking shortly before the bicentennial celebrations in 1976. Or this, still more saliently said: "History does not define us. We define it." That was George W. Bush, speaking shortly after the events of September 11, 2001. In 2012, while campaigning for the presidency, the Republican Mitt Romney faulted President Barack Obama for failing "to shape history"—not history at home, but history in the Middle East, someone else's history.[23]

The historian Richard Hofstadter famously noted that Americans abhorred ideology precisely because America was one.[24] Always, it seems, this is a matter of time and history and where Americans stand in relation to both. It is the core feature of what we now call America's claim to exceptionalism. Anyone professing a belief in such a status, aware of it or not, is expressing a consciousness that is at least partly premodern in character. "However one comes to the debate, there can be little question that the hand of providence has been on a nation which finds a Washington, a Lincoln, or a Roosevelt when it needs him." As the last reference indicates, this is a twentieth-century comment, one delivered in the mid-1990s by the scholar Seymour Martin Lipset. "When I write the above sentence," he added for the sake of clarity, "I believe I draw scholarly conclusions, although I will confess that I write also as a proud American." It may arrive as a confession, but there are the premodern and the modern jostling in a single contemporary soul.[25]

Among the features of exceptionalist thought and sentiment that have sustained it through the centuries, it seems to me, is how simply and frequently Americans confuse history and myth. It is true that history and myth are both forms of narrative. But one is considered valid because it has been properly researched, while the other is useful in providing a clear, uncomplicated idea of one's circumstances. I find this attribute, a certain literal-mindedness in the acceptance of myth as veritable, unusual in the American case. It reflects a dysfunctional relation with history that I will shortly explore. Instead of living in history as all rational human beings understand themselves to be doing, the understanding is that one lives within the timeless myth—constantly renewing and extending it just as if it were lived history.

We see this tendency as early as Winthrop, and it runs through the revolutionary-era literature. The ancient references and the themes of repetition, return, and redemption were plentiful in the telling of the myths, but the myths were nonetheless to constitute a contemporary story and purported to describe events occurring in the modern world. They were not background music so much as the sound of events themselves, the emergent American dialect. They were, in a word, material—inhabited by those disseminating them. This living-within-the-myth bespeaks an extreme self-consciousness, also unusual, in all that America does, at home and among others. It comes to a kind of narcissism. The thought should not be foreign to anyone attentive to American political rhetoric, notably during the American century but also in the decade or so since its close. Who we are and what we are doing and where we are in the great American story are always the implicit subjects.

The first historians to tell the American story appeared during the seventeenth century. They wrote of the days of discovery and settlement, but they wrote with little thought of the historian's profession and often no concern with authorship. The first self-consciously American historians appeared during the revolutionary period. Among these first were David Ramsay, a physician and legislator as well as a historian, and Mrs. Mercy Otis Warren. Mrs. Warren was the descendant of a *Mayflower* passenger and born into a large, prominent Massachusetts family. She was a poet, a playwright, and a vigorous propagandist on the patriotic side. But her surviving work is a history. Warren was nearly fifty when she began *History of the Rise, Progress, and Termination of the American Revolution*. That was in 1775; the three-volume set was completed and published in Boston thirty years later.

Warren set out to write of the present, then, as if it were already past. This was a peculiar thing to attempt at the time. Earlier recorders of the American past had written contemporaneously, but they wrote explorer's logs or records of events they had witnessed or in which they had figured. When the first historians appeared, in the late seventeenth century and early in the eighteenth, they wrote of what had come before. This was Warren's distinction: She wrote of the world around her as history. This tells us other things that are sometimes true about myth: It can be manufactured contemporaneously, and it can represent the ossification of memory. In another time, one might argue, Mrs. Warren may have chosen to serve as a journalist. But the first word of her title was "History," and her intent was plain (and histrionic, fair to say). The present became a kind of instant *illud tempus* in her work, a readymade sacred time.

In Warren we can detect an early example of the impulse to create an identifiably American mode of expression—writing to match the moment's magnitude. But *History of the Rise* is not otherwise accomplished as a work of history or historiographic craft, though it can be read as a document exemplary of its time, and in it one finds numerous of the habits that would characterize the work of noted nineteenth-century historians. Already, not only was the past an imaginary past, but the present was in some measure an imagined present, too. This was Warren's project. Somehow she knew, or intuited, that America would need both as it made its way forward.

There are ferocious battles and "days never to be forgotten by Americans" running through Warren's text. There are barbarities and plunder (British habits); there are zeal, civility, liberal sentiments, and "virtues of native courage" (American virtues, of course). Some of the detail, accurate or otherwise, is gripping. But Warren ended her work in 1805, not long before its publication, on a note that expresses much about Americans and their relations with providential power, time, and history. The passage is remarkable not only for its fidelity to the seventeenth-century vision of the Puritans but also as an early record of the American inheritance as we have it before us—that is, as Americans are now challenged to overcome it.

"And this last civilized quarter of the globe," Warren concluded, may exhibit those striking traits of grandeur and magnificence, which the Divine Oeconomist may have reserved to crown the closing scene, when the angel of his preserve will stand upon the sea and the earth, lift up his hand to heaven, and swear by Him that liveth for ever and ever, that there shall be time no longer.[26]

————

John Adams to Benjamin Rush, a friend and co-signer of the Declaration of Independence; it is 1811, half a dozen years after Warren had completed her master work, three before she expired at eighty-six. The single term Adams had served as president was a decade behind him. Rush was professing medical theory at the University of Pennsylvania. On August 14 Adams wrote:

> For I myself do believe that both tradition and history are already corrupted in America as much as they ever were in the four or five first centuries of Christianity, and as much as they ever were in any age or country in the whole of mankind.

Mrs. Warren would not have been pleased to read these sour words from the irascible, ever-grousing Adams. And Warren may well have known of the former president's sentiments: Adams had been an early and active advocate of her ventures in revolutionary propaganda during their prewar years in Boston.

Rush, in any case, responded in kind. "I have no hesitation," he wrote back five days later, "in expressing a general want of belief not only in tradition but in recorded history and biography. The events of the American Revolution opened my eyes upon these subjects."[27]

What were these two men complaining about? The revolution was but three decades behind them, and they were asserting that its history had been lost, living memory evaporated, and those who had peopled the events of their greatest days already were misunderstood.

We cannot take this exchange simply as one between two aging men unhappy that those younger were not getting it right enough. Warren's *History of the Rise*, indeed, is one symptom of a genuine problem on the minds of the two early statesmen, and she had been among the first to commit the sin. Already by the time of the two men's letters Americans had evinced a love of history. But it was a certain kind of love and a certain kind of history. I term the condition at issue between Adams and Rush—and on full exhibition in Warren's work—history without memory. It is as evident and prevalent among Americans now as it seems to have been in the later days of Adams and Rush.

Americans did not invent the phenomenon of history without memory. It is evident here and there throughout much of the past, particularly in the pasts of great nations and empires. But if Americans did not originate it, they would over time exhibit a somewhat extreme and prolonged case. Why, we must ask. In the beginning there was no need for history because in the framework of American belief—strife, exile, and at last redemption—there was nothing to be learned from the past. What mattered was experience alone. By the twentieth century, history held little interest for the simple reason that there was so much that needed to be left out if the American myths were to be sustained. Myth represents the passage of memory into forgetfulness. And it is in the space left by absent memory that myth settles and thrives and reproduces itself such that it comes to displace history itself.

To live with an abiding affection for the past but with no authentic historical consciousness, no tie to the past as it was, no "historicity"—this is to live in the condition of history without memory. As we have already noted in glossing Warren's work, even as the revolutionary generation lived, it went into history as a saintly population of simple, virtuous people, ever vigorous, ever united in purpose, ever possessed of a "spirit of enterprise," as Warren liked to put it.[28] They have since been borne forward toward us, as a critic wrote at the twentieth century's end, as people who seemed to have just stepped off Noah's Ark. This is history without memory, simply defined: a grand narrative, full of fable.

History without memory is history without time, meaning it is unsusceptible to reinterpretation or change from one generation to the next. It is fixed. This must be so, for its fixedness is essential to maintaining a national mythology. This sometimes obliterates history and sometimes merely romanticizes it. It is filled with "events," but they are "remembered," in quotation marks, and there is no causality (and hence no necessary sequence) binding them. All that happened happened simply "before," for the ever-enveloping present takes the place of the past.

To produce history without memory has its consequences, as Adams and Rush seem to have discerned. It is initially agreeable, particularly for those in power because it has an intimate relationship with power: It enhances and fortifies power. But over time it leaves those producing it and living by it in a certain state of immobility. They are unable to think anew or to imagine a future that is different from the present or the past. A kind of paralysis appears: A people cannot depart from the past they have fabricated by way of a process of omission. From this comes a distortion that creates a barrier to others, and the nation that cannot remember itself comes to be isolated by what evolves into an eccentric insistence upon what was and what was not.

History without memory is not perpetually sustainable. This is counter to the assumptions of those erecting such a history. American officials have shredded many documents and kept many secrets in the manufacture of history without memory during the American century and since its close. But memory cannot be eliminated. It ever triumphs, as countless examples show us. Indeed, the more history is made to exclude it, the more acute memory becomes, the more irritated—and so the more in need of amelioration.

Even as Americans dwelled fondly upon their history they grew ignorant of it, then, for history at a very early moment had begun to take on the character of story—something to be told for the sake of its symmetry and for pleasure and the shapely conveyance of a moral, as against a process that could be understood by way of reflection and historical method. Stories are simple. The nature of the ending is understood beforehand, and they come in the shape of concentric loops, to be told again and again in one form or another. History is none of these things: It is complex and craggy in shape, events occur in it once, there is never a chance of return, the recording of it advances from one generation to the next, and its outcome is never assured.

———

"A happy country without a history," Hegel once wrote of the United States. It was 1826, fifty years after the Declaration had been signed, fifteen since Adams made his grumble to his confidant. Hegel later elaborated the thought in his lectures on history. America was "the land of the future . . . the land of desire for all those who are weary of the historical lumber-room of old Europe."[29] Germans, one cannot be surprised to learn, were especially attentive to this aspect of the new nation across the water. Here are seven lines Goethe wrote on the same theme in 1812:

> America you are more fortunate
> Than our old continent
> You have no ruined castles

And no primordial stones
Your soul, your inner life
Remain untroubled by
Useless memory.[30]

It is easy enough to see why a German philosopher and a German poet of the early nineteenth century would find something enviable in a nation unburdened by a long path into the present. But did America truly have no history, even then? Equally, can memory possibly be so useless as these men seem to have thought? It is more difficult to understand why neither writer appeared to recognize the burden on the dark side of the apparent blessing. By the early nineteenth century Americans had already begun to miss something important about the past and their relation to it and how it should be properly honored. D. H. Lawrence, lots of years later and in another context entirely, put the point as well as anyone in one of his essays. He was writing of the English, but this matters not: He may just as well have written the same words about Americans. "They keep up convention, but they cannot carry on a tradition," Lawrence remarked. "There is a tremendous difference between the two things. To carry on a tradition you must add something to the tradition."[31]

This confused relation with the past was the trap Americans had fallen into by way of their preference for history without memory, and it is useful to dwell upon it because as a nation America has yet to climb out of it. The success of the revolution was taken to mean America had accomplished its great change and was therefore in need of no more of it. But one does not honor the past by refusing to diverge from it. In such a case the past and those who peopled it become the objects of a cult among the living. The American cult of the "Founding Fathers" (always upper-cased, this phrase) is such an example. It is another form of ancestor worship. One honors the past by making something new, something that at first seems to run precisely against the past and the intent of those who came before. Only then has one kept the tradition alive. This point has been elaborated in all manner of places and by all manner of people for the simple reason that it is universal. Another German, writing a little later than Lawrence, cast the thought in terms that seem especially appropriate to the American case, though he may or may not have had Americans at all in mind. "Whenever man imagined he had found 'eternal beauty' he fell back into imitation and stagnation," the architect Walter Gropius once noted. "True tradition is the result of constant growth. Its quality must be dynamic, not static, to serve as an inexhaustible stimulus to man."[32]

Was serving as such a stimulus not America's most abiding ambition—its largest? Do many Americans not continue to profess this as the national ambition today?

———

To cultivate the condition of history without memory is vitally important if one is intent on living by way of a mythological past. So is the ossification of tradition. The use of stories is one way this is accomplished. Museums, monuments, and a large variety of "sites of memory" are others. And, paradoxically enough, history in the American mode requires that stories and historical sites are rendered with a great veracity, often with an almost compulsive attention to detail. The events portrayed actually occurred just as depicted, an American reading a popular history, or someone watching a historical drama on television, is able to say with confidence. That is how they went into battle. That is how the room looked. That is how they sounded and, most of all, how they felt.

This is the storylike fashion in which Americans like to take their history. It is primarily a visual style: What did it look like? Let us see the faces; show us just where it happened. This is why popular histories and biographies by American masters of these genres are painted with the same impasto and lit with the same dramatic glow as eighteenth-century landscapes and portraits. It is why so many Americans are drawn to re-created colonial towns such as Williamsburg, in Virginia, or villages such as Sturbridge, in Massachusetts. These are re-creations of how things once were—visual, material representations. They give a certain sensation not only of knowing "how it was" but also of participating in how it was, walking around in how it was, feeling how it was—but not, it must be said, of understanding how it was.

It is the same with the American habit of "reenacting." We have revolutionary-era reenactors, Civil War reenactors, Wild West reenactors, Vietnam war reenactors, and so on. It is hard to think of anyone else who takes their history in so tactile a manner. Reenacting—the uniforms, the muskets, the brass buttons, the precise knowledge of hills and stone walls and riverbanks and what happened at each—this is something few but Americans seem to have a taste for. And it seems to be only Americans who are dedicated to the details of discrete stories so as to avoid history with true memory—history as it is made of an infinite, unshapely, and unmanageable maze of events that arose from an infinite number of decisions and choices with the same infinite number of motivations behind them. What is so often missing is the cause and effect of history, the human agency, and hence a true narrative.

And here lies the paradox: All the veracity and detail to which so much of the telling of American history is given comes, in the end, to the abstraction of history itself. One is relieved of any obligation to comprehend history's meaning. It is with an excessive closeness that so many Americans elude the larger story known truly as history and the way of understanding our moment known as historical consciousness. And it is by way of this abstracting that the habit of taking history without memory survives, as alive in our time as it was in Mercy Warren's.

An imaginary, mythological past requires the unceasing production of an imaginary present. We find this today in our military's occasional attempts to fabricate heroes, to take a familiar instance. We find it in our government's incessant tampering with and destruction of records. This amounts to the sacking of history. There is plentiful imagery available to all of us, a function of the technology at our disposal to disseminate the images. There are also our portrayals of others—our "evil empire" and our "axis of evil" and our "Islamofascism." Each one is a mirror in which America's virtue is reflected. All of this will suffuse the history of our time, leaving it blurred, and giving many chores to historians dedicated to a clear, coherent accounting of things.

In the beginning rhetoric was foremost among the devices used to maintain the present in mythological time. There are other ways at the enterprise now, but rhetoric remains as important today as it was in 1630 or 1775. It is possible that Ronald Reagan is now better known for his rhetorical invocations of the "City upon a Hill" than Winthrop himself. Reagan made use of the imagery at least twice— once when accepting his party's presidential nomination in 1984 and again in his farewell address to the nation five years later. What was Reagan invoking in those moments, we have to ask. What are we invited to remember when we remember them: history, as Reagan pretended to understand it, or the history of a nation with, as Hegel surmised, no history—a nation with (Hegel again) only desires and a dream?

A CULTURE OF REPRESENTATION

As soon as histories are properly told there
will be no more need of romances.
—Whitman, *Leaves of Grass*, 1855

There was a moment in Theodore Roosevelt's life that was of epiphanic importance. It seems so, at least, according to a correspondent who witnessed it and to the many historians and biographers who have since drawn on the account Edward Marshall of the *New York Journal* wrote afterward.

It was June 24, 1898, Roosevelt's third day in Cuba with his already-famous Rough Riders. They had come to a craggy ridgeline called Las Guásimas, behind which a few hundred Spanish troops had taken up a rear-guard position. With a detachment of American regulars ahead of him coming under heavy fire, Roosevelt rushed his men forward through a patch of dense jungle and over a fence made of rusted barbed wire. A dozen or so had crossed ahead of their stout, forty-year-old commander.

"Then he stepped across the wire himself," wrote Marshall (who took a bullet at Las Guásimas that left him paralyzed). "It was as if that barbed-wire strand had formed a dividing line in his life, and that when he stepped across it he left behind him in the path all those unadmirable and conspicuous traits which have so often caused him to be justly criticized in civic life, and found on the other side of it, in that Cuban thicket, the coolness, the calm judgment, the towering heroism, which made him, perhaps, the most admired and best beloved of all Americans in Cuba."[1]

Cool, calm, towering, the leaving behind of all past shortcomings: However we may judge the objectivity of this passage, it purports to describe Roosevelt's first moments on the foreign battleground he had desired for many years to tread. Las Guásimas lasted but an hour by Roosevelt's watch (two, according to others), and it ended in a rout for the invaders of the Spanish empire. The enemy, by one account, scattered "like ants shaken from a biscuit."[2] This was not a great surprise. Spain's crumbly colonies did not make for much of an adversary, as TR famously observed beforehand, but they would have to do: for him and for America, given his thought that both were in need of a war.

Las Guásimas, lying along Cuba's southern coast, was also the first moment of overseas combat for American soldiers during what we now call the American century. And the coincidence between the personal story and the national story could not but have gratified Roosevelt. He often made much of the straight-line similarities between his own transformative experiences and those of the United States. The Spanish-American War—finished in five months, both Roosevelt and his nation changed forever—was a near-perfect example of what he meant.

He was frail and sickly as a child—nothing like the man he was to become. As all Roosevelt's biographers note, he was asthmatic, of nervous disposition, withdrawn, bespectacled by thirteen. In all, what comes through in the accounts is a kind of Fauntleroy with a bookish aspect. Then came a moment of decision, it seems, a leaving behind and a going forward not unlike the crossing of the barbed wire. At eleven Roosevelt set out on an apparently rigorous regime to remake himself, physically and within. A gymnasium was built in the family's mansion just off Fifth Avenue in New York. "You must *make* your body," Roosevelt later recalled his father counseling. He practiced fearlessness, he said later, until "it changes from pretense to reality."[3]

By his mid-teens Roosevelt was robust, the asthma was in retreat, and the cult of assertive manliness and self-mastery that would mark him out all his life had begun to emerge. So had a notable need to prove himself, especially (though not only) in all matters physical and material. Harvard followed, then a first taste of politics in New York, and then his celebrated (if brief) adventure in cattle ranching in what was at the time the Dakota Territory. He arrived in the summer of 1883, just turning twenty-five and wearing a buckskin-fringed suit—the perfect "dude" out from the East. The legend was in the making, unadmirable and conspicuous habits included, and most of it would be made by the purposeful hand of the young man "preparing to do the rough work of the world."[4]

It was rather the same for the United States, Roosevelt considered. It had been a youthfully unsteady republic at the start, uncertain of itself and fearful of enemies. By the accounts of some historians, it was a touch self-conscious as to its possibly effeminate sensibilities when faced with the great, assertive powers of Europe. But during the nineteenth century it had "made its own body," so to say, and emerged (at least in the material sphere) a nation to contend with any among the imperial powers. It was time, by Roosevelt's day, for America to step out of the gymnasium and show the world its strength—to begin practicing its fearlessness, bring America's manliness into sharp relief, and take its rightful place. Scarcely was Roosevelt the only one to see things this way, but this is what the Spanish empire meant to him: a doddering, decrepit remnant but enough in its defeat to put America on a map that spanned two oceans.

The reticent William McKinley, elected president in the momentous political contest of 1896, gave little thought to such matters as physical prowess or brute strength during his somewhat sedentary life. He was concerned with his personal dignity—this seems to have nearly obsessed him—and with preserving an old, hopelessly fading idea of America as it had been bred into him across the farmlands and small towns of his native Ohio. He seems to have cared more for keeping America one than he did for imperial adventures. He equivocated over going to war for many months before a riotously war-mongering press, the swell of public opinion, and the views of Roosevelt and others around him forced his hand in April 1898. Spain declared war on the twenty-fifth. Washington followed on the same day (backdating its diplomatic note to the twenty-third).

Then McKinley made an interesting decision, one suggesting that his thinking resembled Roosevelt's in at least one aspect. America would raise a new army to take on Spain, McKinley declared, one hundred and twenty-five thousand volunteers in all. And three of its regiments would be reserved for men of the West, the frontiersmen who had lived and worked on and, indeed, made America's outward flank. Eight years earlier the census bureau in Washington had declared the frontier gone: There was no more of it left. The war with Spain would show Americans something different. There were frontiers to be conquered beyond the continental frontier, a West beyond the West as Americans had always thought of it, and things to get done in places that would be new frontiers. For the next hundred years, America would never want for one.

Once McKinley made up his mind about the cavalry of cowboys, it was instantly evident around Washington that Roosevelt was the man to head it. He demurred when offered the title of colonel—he was formally named second-in-command—but all involved knew, as did anyone who read a newspaper, that the Rough Riders would be his. At least by way of his persona, he, too, was a man of the West, imbued with the true American character and spirit. Roosevelt resigned as assistant secretary of the navy and received his lieutenant-colonel's commission on May 6. Nine days later he arrived in Texas to train his troops. The camp was a fairground outside of San Antonio. This time he wore a uniform custom-tailored at Brooks Brothers: a light tan with trim a bright yellow.

———

Relatively speaking, at least, Roosevelt was ever after modest about his first outing on a battlefield. He seems to have done well, but he admitted later to a certain amateur's confusion. He fired at anything that was not a tree; at one point, isolated from the army regulars, he longed for his superior officer to send him orders. "I had an awful time trying to get into the fight and trying to do what was right when in it," he wrote later, "and all the while I was thinking that I was the only man who did not know what I was about."[5]

He was far from this, either in Cuba or at home. Even amid the American public's compulsive lust for war, a certain foreboding appears to have lingered beneath the surface of public life. At times the historical accounts suggest something near to a nationally shared premonition, as if everyone knew that something more than a fight with an encrusted empire was about to begin. The temporizing McKinley gave voice to this as well as anyone. "Who knows where this war will lead us?" he asked as he made his preparations. "It may be more than a war with Spain."[6] To a confidant shortly before he asked Congress for a war declaration, he fretted for the future. "The country should understand," he said, "that we are striving to make our course consistent not alone for today, but for all time."[7] This was accurate enough as a reflection of the public disposition. No sooner had Congress made the war official, Roosevelt observed, than "our people . . . fell into a condition of panic apprehension as to what the foe might do."[8]

As to Roosevelt himself, he never lost his taste for appearances—the way things ought to look. And in the tropical jungle, with the weird buzz of Mauser bullets all around him, he did something both odd and humorous as he helped lead the American charge into the wider world. He insisted on wearing a saber, as so many great soldiers had done since the revolution and through the Civil War. As an evocation of another age it proved a troublesome reference, for it kept getting tangled in the thick bush of the Cuban countryside, causing Roosevelt no end of annoyance, though he persisted with it to the end at Las Guásimas. In speeches long afterward, and in the book he wrote on his experience in the war, Roosevelt once again tried to make slightly light of his own vanity. "I never wore it again in action," he wrote of his saber in *The Rough Riders*, "as it kept getting between my legs when I was tearing my way through the jungle."[9]

This was America on the eve of its century: full of itself to the point of bursting, highly conscious of its image and the need to appear strong, a little lost amid the old European world of slow diplomacy and balance-of-power politics, and altogether ill at ease as to what exactly it was embarking upon. Power and anxiety, which would soon become a peculiarly American combination, were on full display. Stephen Crane caught the same premonitory mood on the Cuban front, where he was writing for the *New York World*. In

Wounds in the Rain, the book he published on the war in 1900, he wrote of an eerie apprehension he saw in the Americans as they assembled to support local rebels. It was as if those soldiers, more than McKinley or anyone else, had unwittingly positioned themselves to peer briefly into all that was to come from the Spanish war onward. "Contrary to the Cubans, the bronze faces of the Americans were not stolid at all," Crane wrote in a passage of extraordinary cogency. "One could note the presence of a curious expression—something dreamy, the symbol of minds striving to tear aside the screen of the future and perhaps expose the ambush of death."[10]

———

It is curious to reflect upon a few of the countless details available to us now as to how the American century began. What can we learn from the small decisions and incidents in the lives of large, prominent Americans? Why do we find alike in the timorous, nostalgic McKinley and the ever-ebullient Roosevelt the same preoccupation with imagery and reenactment? Why did Americans enter the American century within a frame of reference that consistently arose out of what had happened in the past? They made of Cuba a stage set to be filled with cowboys and officers heir to a storied, magisterial military past. What does it tell us that events were understood by these men not as they were but as representations that awarded them some resonant meaning beyond their meaning?

Everything that occurred at this momentous time, including the war itself, seemed validated for its aspect of reiteration. Sabers in the jungle, frontiersmen shipped to the Cuban countryside, that curious mix of war fever and a tremulous diffidence: Did it all suggest, somehow, a reply to the world—the modern world as it was then arriving—a world Americans eagerly embraced, on the one hand, and on the other one they were not sure they understood and therefore dreaded?

I mean to suggest by these too-many questions that America, when it launched into the century that would take its name, entered fully into what I propose calling a culture of representation. Simply put, a culture of representation is one dedicated to interpretation as a primary impulse. It is always at a remove from reality. It strips all events of politics, for there can be none in the representational dimension. Few large events have meaning in and of themselves; most things and events in the present are assigned allusive meanings, and these legitimize them as foreordained echoes of what had come before. This is why a representational culture admits of no genuine politics or dissent: To engage in either is to dispute what is beyond dispute—the shared beliefs, feelings, and assumptions from which a common identity is made. Representation is at bottom an instrument of power. To represent elevates him or her who is representing before those watching. A certain aura is assumed, a certain authority. Representation of this kind confers a higher value, perhaps a sacred or mythical value, on what he or she who is representing does. It calls upon earlier greatness, real or imagined, for there is always a "before"—remembered or "remembered" or merely conjured—in a culture of representation. This culture tends to keep the gaze fixed behind. So it is also a culture of nostalgia, a culture of reference.[11]

Representation can be closely associated with myth. This is so when one purports to act within the myth. The image presented is not merely an image—it is the very thing depicted, a renewal of the myth. And those who accept the representation are unable to distinguish, so far as meaning is concerned, between the original myth and the reiteration. In the American case, Roosevelt and those around him depended on two myths to get the war with Spain up and running. One was America's worldly mission, its destiny to bring liberty to the world. The other was a new myth, for the nineteenth century had just recently been mythologized: This was the myth of the lone individual pushing America's frontier ever outward. From this moment onward American individualism (as an "ism") would not be separable from the nation's idea of its worldly mission.

This was America's heritage, its inheritance, for we find in the American past that extraordinary continuity in the national mythology and ideology. From Winthrop and the Puritans onward styles of representation were one way, an important way, for America to understand itself. Mercy Otis Warren's *History of the Rise* was an act of representation more than it was a history book. What distinguishes 1898 is in part the American determination to carry the culture of representation across an ocean—that is, to present it to others beyond its borders. The war with Spain was our first attempt to take old values—a worldly mission and the frontier spirit—and declare them as a new myth. Something not altogether rational was awakened in the American psyche that spring. America had begun to speak in a slightly different tongue. Others could not, thenceforth, understand America without understanding that it was engaged in representing itself to itself without reference to anything outside of it. The nation's culture of representation, to put the point another way, became a determinant for a century of human history.

Representation assumed another new dimension in 1898. It was to become pervasive, and it was to be deployed as a defense against the arriving modern. The world and all that happened in it did not have to be understood as it presented itself, for there was another, pre-modern frame of reference that could be set against it. This gave representation an abstract aspect. No longer would it reference what was in ideal form: It became a "re-presentation" of what was no longer and would never be again. A modern culture of representation is thus revealed as a culture of longing, for it arises precisely at the moment when that alluded to has passed into the past. And this was America at the nineteenth century's conclusion: lost to its pastoral past, lost to its frontier, unsure of what would or how to replace either of them.

There are consequences of this way of seeing the world and one's place in it. These are what must interest us today. To impose interpretation on one's decisions and policies and acts means one is liable to see things not as they are; by definition one is open to misinterpretation. One is prone, yet more, to a disproportionate view of one's place among others. With a people's gaze fixed backward, the present bears no legitimacy of its own and the future is invisible. There is a givenness, finally, to a certain kind of narcissism and a certain kind of paranoia. A. N. Whitehead put the point as succinctly as anyone in the lectures he published on symbolism in 1927—lectures he had delivered to an American audience. "Symbolic reference is very fallible," the English philosopher wrote. "It may induce actions, feelings, emotions, and beliefs about things which are mere notions without that exemplification in the world which the symbolism leads us to presuppose."[12]

These habits of mind among Americans beg exploration, then, for they are all, to one degree or another and to one result or another, features of America's idea of itself during the American century. A culture of representation has much to do with the thought that America's hundred and three years in the sun may have to be judged as near or nearer to failure as to success. "The life of humanity," Whitehead warned, "can easily be overwhelmed by its symbolic accessories." It is difficult to avoid seeing something of America's fate in this remark. Here or there the nation misinterpreted, or overinterpreted, or failed to see, or failed simply to care what was available to see, because it was too taken by its own representation of itself as humanity's highest achievement, the world's redeemer.

"This is not to be a hippodrome affair," Roosevelt grandly advised a *New York Times* reporter as he entrained for the fairground in

San Antonio to prepare his troops for battle.[13] The assertion deserves a moment's thought. Did it refute or suggest a givenness to theater, to masquerade, among those who can be counted, more or less, the founding fathers of the century to which America would soon enough give its name?

———

Confining ourselves to the Atlantic world, it is not too much to say that the nineteenth century belonged to Europe, not America. One can even suggest that America did not have a nineteenth century in any but a few important respects. It had something closer to a prolonged version of the eighteenth. This would prove, during what we call the American century, a fateful missing out. More than anything else, America would be underexposed and come very late to the currents of thought—political, social, economic, aesthetic, philosophical, and most of all historical—that carried the rest of the Western world into the modern era.

Yes, the new nation prospered as its founders had hoped. Jefferson's farmers multiplied and pressed westward at an astonishing pace; Hamilton had his banks and industry and urban commerce. Later on, Henry Clay got significant parts of his "American System" into place. But only one of the truly great events of the century following the two great revolutions of the late 1700s took place on American soil. The nineteenth century was one of tremendous advances for humanity. But all these advances occurred in Europe. The single exception was the Civil War, for the ground it broke would eventually bear much fruit.

Why was this? Why did the nineteenth century find its center in the old world and not the new?

Good historians tell us that we can trace the seminal thinking and events of the nineteenth century onward from the mid-eighteenth. Montesquieu published *The Spirit of the Laws* in 1748; Adam Smith's

Wealth of Nations followed in 1776, promising a harmonious, progressive social order that was to emerge out of the freeing of the individual and the laws of liberal markets—both advanced as states of nature, not to be improved upon. Over the next decade Condorcet published his celebrated treatise on the nature of human progress and J. G. Herder his *Ideas Toward a Philosophy of History.* These writers were exemplary of the forward edge of their time. It would be difficult to overstate the importance of what they did so much to begin: the gradual discovery of human society as a phenomenon to be studied and considered in, of, and for itself. This was the modern world, as we now understand the term, irrupting through the surface of time at last. True, many eighteenth-century thinkers were still in search of unchanging laws—"the immutable law of right," as Condorcet put it, a secularized version of the divine law out of which they were emerging. But time and history were coming ever closer to the earth by way of such men—ever down from any divine law determined and passed to humanity from behind the clouds.

———

Following the works of the eighteenth century's great thinkers, and concurrently with a few of them, the French Revolution pushed Europe into a state of crisis and confusion that no one alive today could ever understand in the fullness of its sensation. It is impossible because we have never lived through a comparably tumultuous passage—not yet, at any rate, and not in the West. All was suddenly uncertain, all things and events without apparent foundation.

The critical feature of 1789, the aspect of it that made it so determining of the fate of Europe, is easily stated. The French failed. All the hope and expectation and millennial aspiration that so many Europeans had invested in the revolution would have to be cast forward as something still to be awaited and something decidedly secular, for the revolution itself had come to nothing more than tyranny and reaction. Life and society and all that drove them would have to be reconsidered.

What is more, life and society were changing at an extraordinary pace. Early industrialization had already begun to produce differentiated classes, each with its interests, each opposed to others. So had the infallible laws of free markets and exchange led to something other than the harmonious society that Smith and the Scottish liberals seemed to have promised. All that had so recently been simple took on a new complexity; all that had for so long appeared changeless was suddenly in incessant flux.

This condition of crisis was prolonged and acute all at once. Auguste Comte, who conceived of what we know now as modern sociology, was born in 1798 and had lived through four different political regimes by the time he was eighteen years old. He was one of many to determine that Europe's multiplying postrevolutionary dilemmas were not material but philosophic—existential, as we might now say. "The great political and moral crisis that societies are now undergoing," he wrote when still young, "is shown by a rigid analysis to arise from intellectual anarchy."[14] Of what did society consist? What drove it forward—what laws, what principles? How should it be ordered and managed? Was the past to be discarded in its entirety? These questions suggest the anarchy requiring the rigid analysis Comte argued for. It was up to humankind, suddenly, to solve humankind's problems and failings and—far from least—to understand its past and construct its future. Among Europe's discoveries during this century was that to understand oneself in time is crucial to developing one's political and social thought. Time is the medium of all human encounters.

This milieu has left its stamp on European thinking. It was in it that what we now know as the social sciences—political science and moral philosophy at the outset, then sociology, economics, and history—grew expansively from their eighteenth-century roots. Comte's *Cours de philosophie positive,* published in the 1830s and 1840s, was a foundational text, but many others accompanied it, and one school branched off another or took as its starting point an opposition to what had come before it. Comte set out in search of the laws of social progress that lay beneath history. He opposed the liberal capitalism of the time. By way of scientific rationality, Comte asserted, humankind could understand the workings of its social environments and act upon them. In this we find a seed of social democracy. Comte's was a historical view: He expected the future to reflect more elevated versions of the traditional organic societies of the past. Marx looked through history, too, but he saw differently. Capitalism was a destructive stage in it, and at its far end, after its final stage, it was socialism that would bring society back into a harmonious state. Herbert Spencer, a liberal, looked forward to an industrial society that was as cooperative as it was competitive.

All of these contending social and philosophic schools, from the late-eighteenth-century thinkers through Marx, John Stuart Mill, Spencer, and many others, shared certain beliefs and assumptions. They all took social progress as a given: Humankind was advancing. They were all dedicated to a search for the laws that must lie beneath the surface of events and therefore govern them: natural laws, scientific laws, the law of progress itself, the law of human reason. This was an expression of confidence and anxiety all at once. Nineteenth-century thinkers in Europe shared a new belief in the validity of scientific investigation, on the one hand. At the same time, many of these thinkers, notably those working in the early years of the new century, had embarked on an almost desperate search for something to replace the divine law previously thought to rule human events.

One feature of the early nineteenth century in Europe marked it off from the past more significantly than any other. The French

Revolution and the upheavals that followed it began to tilt Europeans toward a new conception of time and history. The latter would at last be understood as a human construction. It was determined and made by the societies humankind formed and was sustained by humanly made structures of power. Human agency, in short, was all there was to shape earthly events. This plunged European society rather abruptly into time as most of us now ordinarily think of it. In this way, Europe made the nineteenth century the century of history.

The process I describe in brief was complex, filled with currents and crosscurrents, and did not occur quickly. It was only by the mid-nineteenth century that historicism, as scholars term it, had firmly taken hold. And before and after that point, there was lingering resistance to the implications of the historicist understanding of human events. Historicism, as used here, denotes a shift in perspective such that events are understood via their context—their past, their place, their geography, the culture in which they occurred. Historicism is worldly, it is humanist, it is innately social as against individualist, and it would stand against eternal Christian time. But even as historicism emerged, its consciousness of complexity, contingency, and historical context did not put an end to the search for underlying laws that were presumed to govern society and which could be relied upon to be as immutable as God's law had once been taken to be. The implication of Spencer's work, for instance, was that humanity advanced deterministically according to natural laws and that history's course was more or less preset. Spencer, indeed, ridiculed history as nothing more than the gathering of stories concerning monarchs and their wars.

The embrace of history as humanity's alone to make was, then, qualified for many years. In time, however, and with German historicists in the lead, all was subject to historical probity and analysis. Nothing, in the end, was left immune from the historian's researches, for all that had ever occurred on earth was understood to be worthy of a historically rooted reconsideration. In 1863 the French historian Ernest Renan published *The Life of Jesus,* a not untypical endeavor in its time. Renan had already been much influenced by the German historicists, which was also not uncommon. He went on to write a five-volume history of the people of Israel—in effect taking on the Bible. "I consider it as probable that there was a *midrasch* [a story, a study] upon the life of Moses," Renan wrote, "in which nearly all the data of the Sacred History were taken up, blunted, and loaded with fabulous incidents after the captivity."[15] The passage is representative of Renan's assumptions and ambitions.

Such works also exemplify the true advance of the nineteenth century as I describe it. In my view, the most significant event, if it can be considered singly, of the entire postrevolutionary period in the West was the advance of human consciousness into modernity and history, an advance against forgetting and an advance against mythological or providentially inspired interpretations of the human story. This was the humanization of history. And as a human endeavor it belonged to Europeans. The century of history was theirs. They had changed, most fundamentally, themselves. So did those who lost in the age of revolution go on to gain much—not easily, not without great struggle—in the age that followed.

———

It did not take long for the social and political fermentation of Europe in the first half of the nineteenth century to reach American shores. America is commonly understood to have entered an inward-turned period of isolation after the dramatic years of its birth, but this should not be exaggerated. There was traffic, there was travel, there was much study abroad.

Nonetheless, it is true that Europe's emerging disciplines were put to profoundly different purposes once they arrived across the ocean, for they were imports from what was already foreign territory. Americans and Europeans looked upon the world very differently by the early 1800s, and the reason for this is once again simple: Just as the French had failed, the American experiment had proven out with the defeat of the British. The new world was truly something new—a claim to success no European could make.

It is odd to think of how the new sciences of society were absorbed and taught in a land that had little need of them. The rectitude and values of the Puritans had been borne forward on America's pulpits and through its new industrial culture. This was a vestige of an archaic strain in the European consciousness—a sensibility in flight from the modern. Time was still sacred time in the new nation; human events depended on the providential hand. America had inherited "the liberal fragment," as the scholar Louis Hartz put it, and classical liberalism, Locke's liberalism, was sufficient. What need for sociology or political economy?

The new disciplines were initially taught, then, as loosely conceived subsets of moral philosophy and Christian learning. Instruction took place in institutions (available to the few) that were overseen by the clerical elite. And what attracted lecturers most were laws that governed all of nature and could be taken, thus, as divine laws made manifest on the earthly plane. The purveyors of higher learning were particularly drawn to those ideas that did not disrupt American institutions and presuppositions: the eternal republic, the exceptional nation, the liberal market. And to dissent from these teachings was, from a quite early date, to be somehow "un-American," for to dissent was to call into question the whole of the American project.

An entry in a philosophic encyclopedia in the mid-twentieth century describes the intellectual climate of antebellum America as consisting of stagnant air and a dogmatic torpor.[16] There was more to the period than this, we now know, but these do not seem wholly unfair terms. This does not mean there was no such thing as progress during the new nation's first decades. Far from it, of course. It means simply that it was measured differently. Americans did not think of it as located in advances toward a deeper understanding of social, political, or economic phenomena. They felt no need to. Progress was spatial rather than temporal, and it was emphatically material. America had been through its great phase of change when it had its revolution. Thenceforth, change would be quantitative—changes in degree—rather than qualitative, changes in human and worldly relations, in knowledge and politics, in historical understanding and thought. These were what change and progress meant in Europe. Only a small, well-to-do elite in America understood this.

It would be difficult to match Henry Adams for his description of Americans as they gathered their strength and resources during the middle decades of the nineteenth century. In a few brief sentences in his autobiography he managed to evoke both the dynamism of Americans and, side by side, their aversion to the intellectual complexities coursing through Europe. "The new Americans," he wrote in *The Education of Henry Adams*, "must, whether they were fit or unfit, create a world of their own, a science, a society, a philosophy, a universe, where they had not yet created a road or even learned to dig their own iron." And then:

> They had no time for thought; they saw and could see nothing beyond their day's work. . . . Above all, they naturally and intensely disliked being told what to do, and how to do it, by men who took their ideas and their methods from the abstract theories of history, philosophy, or theology. They knew enough to know that their world was one of energies quite new.[17]

This is an incisive distinction between Europe and America and what progress meant on either side of the ocean. Americans had a lively nineteenth century, full of progress in its own meaning of the term, full of "new energies." The cotton gin, the steamboat, the wheat combine, the telegraph: All of these came before 1850 and were the sorts of punctuation marks Americans preferred in the measuring of time and the telling of the story as it went on. They all had to do with the taming of land and the managing of distance. But the change such inventions brought is what we mean by quantitative change as against qualitative, and the resource to which Americans devoted themselves was space—land—as against time or history. And as I have already suggested, the truly profound advances of the nineteenth century were not material. Europeans had changed the European self; change in America meant change in the physical world. In this way, just as the defeated in the eighteenth century went on to great advances, the victors during the revolutionary era lost out on much in the century that came after it.

————

But what about the new nation's historians, the scholar-writers who gave Americans the intellectual bedrock of their narrative, the stuff of a new nation's conversation? If America dwelled outside of time, of what did the historian's craft consist? Those of the nineteenth century were the first to think self-consciously of creating an American tradition in the writing of history. Of what would this tradition be made? It is, after all, a tradition that survives among us, even if an alternative tradition has arisen to take a prominent place beside it.

The nineteenth-century historians considered great are names that come down to us more or less familiarly: Francis Parkman, William Prescott, John Motley, George Bancroft. These are generally accepted as high among the figures of the American tradition as that tradition took root during what was long considered (for who can guess what reason) history's "golden age" in America. They chose diverse subjects, for a time not even American subjects, as if to make the point that history was elsewhere and America outside of it. Parkman wrote about the American wilderness, but that was a breakthrough accomplishment at the time—and was in a certain way "other" to his readers in any case. Prescott made the Spanish empire his specialty, and Motley the Dutch. Bancroft, the standout in this group, the most ambitious and zealous bearer of the American past forward, wrote a sweeping history of revolutionary America commencing "from the discovery of the American continent." But even as they went different ways, it is remarkable to consider all these men had in common—and hence the shared idea of history advanced in their books.

All of them, and most other historians of their time, came from Boston and had the same notion of New England's special mission—to preserve and advance the American miracle—at the core of their thinking. To look out at the world from Beacon Hill was to see it from humanity's highest station. They were all greatly taken by the Romantic movement in Europe, though they all, one way or another, drew inspiration from the soil of their own nation. Equally, all the giants of the time had backgrounds in either literature or the ministry—and sometimes both. Parkman and Prescott wrote novels and literary essays before turning to history; Bancroft wrote poetry and trained for the Unitarian ministry.

The historians of what many consider the classical American period were, then, classic New England men of letters, and for them history was at its core a literary pursuit—far from the social science it was becoming in Europe. Not for them "a philosophic theme" (Prescott) or "mere abstract ideas or unsubstantial images" (Parkman). That kind of history was for the irreverent, God-mocking Germans and those they had influenced. The Americans, by contrast, believed in the historicity of miracles. They wanted "epics in prose" (Prescott again) and "a pictured, illuminated past" (Motley). Above all, history had to hold "interest, interest, interest," as Prescott wrote in a memorandum to himself.[18]

Interesting, interesting, interesting is a merciless landlord, as any writer knows, and it made for a certain kind of history. It suggested a conception of history as story—an idea of the discipline still all too alive among us. By way of method the classical historians drew from painters and poets more than they did from thinkers. They got more from Rubens and Sir Walter Scott than they ever would from Herder, Hegel, or any of the other Germans. They used landscape, portraiture, and immense amounts of detail to produce color, vitality, character—the last was a must—and all was to be arranged into shapely narrative forms.

The desired effects were in essence appeals to the emotions. These historians wanted to prick the reader's imagination, producing in him or her a sense of verisimilitude, of being there, of participating in the action. In a word history was to be embodied rather than dissected and interpreted. It was reenactment in writing to the extent that this could be achieved. Parkman and Bancroft made it a point to visit the sites that would figure in their books. Parkman explained what he was after in *Montcalm and Wolfe,* one of his better-known efforts: "The emotions of a buried and forgotten past."[19]

———

History as arrangement comes to history without memory, and the undesired effects the classical historians achieved (if this is the word) were not infrequently as numerous as the desired. A later critic wrote that he considered Parkman's productions halfway to fictions. Parkman is noted today for the egregious prejudices that mar his work: He went, for instance, from the Native American as the noble savage to simply the savage as the books went on.

Equally, this approach to history tended to produce conventions. There were stock characters, landscapes, and clear, bright skies as signifiers. There were layers of unsupported adjectives, the effect of which was not unlike an overdone chintz. The detail may have been profuse, but it was also selected to suit the story. Inaccuracy, given the need for morally uplifting outcomes, was bound to appear frequently, and it did. Bancroft considered that if a direct quotation was evocative of a character but did not quite fit the passage, then the quotation would have to be bent to do its work.

Bancroft is by far the most interesting of the classical historians. It was he more than any other who delivered the nineteenth-century tradition nearly to the doorstep of the twentieth. The Bancroft Prize remains among the great honors an American historian can earn. And while his style is antiquated—and was so nearly as soon as he finished his work—it is easy to detect his footprint today in our most popular portraitists and narrators of the American past. The light that lit his work often lights theirs: the light of "faithful patriotism," to take a phrase from the opening of Bancroft's monumental *History of the United States, from the Discovery of the American Continent,* the twelve-volume work to which he devoted nearly a half-century of his lengthy life.

It is extraordinary to explore the pages of this work today, knowing its popularity during Bancroft's lifetime and the honor his name still bestows. It soars in its triumphalism and drips with detail—"Hearts glowed warmly on the banks of the Patapsco"—that the historian could not possibly have confirmed.[20] He took evident delight in describing "the glory of this New World," and settlers west of the Alleghenies "accepting from nature their title deeds to the unoccupied wilderness."

The will and work of God, indeed, are never far away in Bancroft. "And why should man organize resistance to the grand design of Providence!" he exclaimed in one of his many high notes. "Why should not the consent of the ancestral land and the gratulations of every other call the young nation to its place among the powers of the earth?"

There are many hundreds of pages of the kind of material that draws one's attention to "the prosperity of our Jerusalem," to choose another phrase nearly at random. At times excesses such as these make the work of Mercy Otis Warren, who wrote of the American Revolution contemporaneously, seem the soberest of balanced accounts. Filled with "intrepid souls," America in Bancroft's lengthy rendering is "the finest country and the happiest climate on the globe."

He was a curious figure. His years make an oddly symmetrical frame for his century: He was born in 1800 and died at ninety-one—at the very edge of his own outdating. He was of an old Massachusetts family and had taken his Unitarian training seriously, but his love of literature—not history, precisely—won out as the man emerged from the young man. Yet more interesting, this most American of historians spent two years in Göttingen, seat of one of Germany's great universities and a center for the new German historicism. From his professors Bancroft wanted to acquire method, technique—the only things all young nations seem to want from those older. Method he could bring home and put to use in evoking and certifying the American spirit, his elders advised him. But he was not to bear back any Continental skepticism or godlessness. Such were not to contaminate his literary sensibility.

Bancroft published the first three volumes of his *History* while still in his thirties. Method and technique did not distinguish them. What stood out onward from his first sentences was less his thinking about America than his boundless, uncritical belief in it. However much America had advanced, Bancroft considered, it was nothing more than the incessant realization of God's eternal, inalterable intent. Bancroft's story was one of great change with no change at its foundation, given the revolution's providential accomplishment.

The books were instantly in demand. By the time Bancroft completed the work in the 1880s, he would be the most popular historian in America. And his success never seems to have owed much to any secret: Bancroft was simply repeating back to Americans, in exciting detail, the myths and stories they were already inclined to tell themselves—the things they wanted to hear from a learned, authoritative historian, hailing from Boston and with all the right training.

It was in part via Bancroft and his New England colleagues, then, that America could continue, for an implausibly long time, to think of itself as the millennial republic, the beneficiary of divine providence. It was full of intelligent, highly rational people. But this served merely to confirm the belief, for reason was at bottom understood as revelation made flesh: All a good historian might do and decide was so subsumed, the human expression of God's grand plan—the God of Protestant New Englanders, of course.

————

Mainstream American thinking, the reigning ideology, remained pre-historicist until the closing years of the nineteenth century. It is almost shocking to consider that mythically informed histories such as Bancroft's were popular accounts of the American past until the very eve of the twentieth. If we want to talk about America as an isolated, keep-to-itself nation in the nineteenth century, it is in this dimension that the subject is most interesting: It had still not entered history.

Americans now know enough about their past to recognize that many crosscurrents advanced in parallel with the pre-historicist orthodoxy. Nonetheless, the shock of the modern as it began to arrive during the post–Civil War period was precisely such because the orthodoxy had been so prevalent and for so long a period. The offended sensibility, shared by many, was that of the Protestant pastor. It is difficult to absorb the suggestion that one may not be exceptional when all of time and history has been presumed to suggest that one is. Americans alive today should have no trouble understanding this: It is almost exactly their dilemma. And this is why the period between the sabers of the Civil War that Roosevelt so admired and his advance across the barbed wire at Las Guásimas is worth brief consideration: The conundrum then is an approximate prefiguring of the conundrum now.

———

When we talk about the Gilded Age today, we ordinarily mean the 1890s. But the crisis that came fully into view during that decade, culminating in the war against Spain, had its roots in the Civil War and the quarter of a century that followed it—the Reconstruction period and the tumultuous 1870s and 1880s. It is useful to compare those years with the earlier period in Europe: To some extent, what the French Revolution and its aftermath did to European life and society the Civil War and the ensuing decades did to America.

If there are differences, one of them surely is the shock Americans felt as they were forced by all that was occurring around them to consider the identity upon which their idea of themselves rested. It had become difficult to deny that America was exhibiting the signs of republican decay from which it had until those years assumed immunity. Who are we, they may as well have asked, if God has not singled us out? Is our republic vulnerable, after all, to the same corruption, divisiveness, and decline that have befallen all others? Herbert Spencer, who was influential among American thinkers, had already asserted that progress in complex societies produces varied and not always desirable effects. Was that the law, an altogether earthly law, to which America was also subject?

Many things would have prompted these questions. In the academy, scientific knowledge steadily and speedily eroded the revealed Christian knowledge that had been taught during the antebellum period. This was especially so as Darwin's *Origin of the Species* and Spencer's *First Principles of a New System of Philosophy,* his (pre-Darwinian) application of the theory of evolution to modern society, began to take hold on the American side of the Atlantic in the 1870s. Knowledge and intellectual authority derived from science, not the pulpit—and this is to say positivist science, the science dedicated to discovering and describing phenomena as these can be observed. Out of science, then, one could derive a worldview; a measure of courage attached to the practice of it, for it stood as a refutation of much that had long been accepted. The sciences thus became the instrument by which the clerical elite could be attacked and pushed back, so making room for modern thought and modern disciplines. By the 1870s, Americans were arguing among themselves about the propriety of Christian prayer in public schools.

Beyond the academy, Americans were faced with the disruptive effects of rapid industrialization. Vast social and economic dislocations accompanied this process. Urban centers grew and then grew crowded with new immigrants and the corrupting political machines that arose around them. Money and patronage made their way into politics to an unprecedented extent. Corporations came to tower over the economy. Strikes, violence, political dissent, new political parties based on European thinking—all these signaled the emergence of new wealth and a new and self-evidently permanent American working class with distinct interests of its own. It was a long way, suddenly, from the family farm. And it prompted a new emphasis on realism, which is apparent in even a brief study of the artistic and literary productions of the period, from Winslow Homer to Stephen Crane.

The new realism represented an effort to answer the most critical question of the age. This was the question of America's claim to exceptionalism. A profound sense of discontinuity came with all the change of the Gilded Age crisis. This rupture reinforced a scientific view of events and empirical investigation of them. This was not unique to America. The eve of the twentieth century seems to have jarred loose much of the Western world. But it came especially hard to Americans. America as it was when seen realistically seemed to bear little relation to the America of the past, the America many alive then had grown up presuming to be eternal.

Two relationships of great importance had changed, the one leading to the other. Since its beginning, America had represented humanity in perfect relations with nature. That was where virtue lay. Now, rather suddenly, the American's primary relations were social, with other Americans. Virtue was no longer a given in the emerging America of social beings. The same class consciousness arose as one found in Europe. But it was understood differently. This leads to the question of history. Bancroft was hardly gone before forward-looking historians acknowledged that, yes, America was part of history after all. It lived in time. But it would always be humanity's forward edge and guide, they assured themselves and their readers— so preserving the essential exceptionalism. As to the present, adjustments needed to be made and that was all; corruption and all the rest was no more than a straying from the gifted perfection. Thus was mythical time incorporated into historical time.

It is interesting, from our point of view today, to see where the battle lines were drawn, for they were not so unlike ours. The first generations of social scientists, which arose after the Civil War, took readily to Darwin and Spencer, using their themes as support for the American belief in liberalism: What is is what is meant to be— nothing whatever need be done. It was laissez-faire writ very large and crudely: To contemplate reform was to stand against the laws governing human society. Against these first social scientists came the new Progressive historians. They considered historical time and change carefully; in some respects they opened the American conversation to European thinking for the first time. They wanted to understand the problem of social change, not flinch from it. Society was man's to make, and reform in the present circumstance was essential. But the Progressives were believers, too. They took the transition from communal to industrial America as the last stage of social evolution and the basis for the ideal society America was meant to be. The future held a reformulated utopia, then. We can call this a first experiment in historicism for Americans. But to prolong the exceptionalist myth, instead of stepping out of it, would limit the Progressives' accomplishments. It was in this respect a serious intellectual error.

And against both the social scientists and the historians stood the Protestant evangelicals, whose orthodox utopian sensibilities were the most severely concussed by the 1890s. No, they did not see the matter as having to do with America's entry into history. No, scientific theories imported from across the ocean did not speak to the moment. They saw their time in the well-rehearsed terms to which Americans had always resorted. All the seventeenth-century themes of decay and corruption were sounded as Protestant leaders gazed out upon the newly frenetic eastern cities. For them, there were too many Americans—Americans not of the original American stock: They were not believers, not as Americans had once and reliably been.

These years were an almost apocalyptic passage: The term is not too strong. Much of what occurred was simply outside the boundaries of what American thinking had made comprehensible. Given the way Americans had spent the nineteenth century, they were not equipped to interpret themselves or any purpose for themselves in a modern idiom. The questions were the old questions: Would America fulfill its destiny as humanity's torchbearer, or would this vision collapse beneath the gathering threats to it? Plainly America needed to be defended "as the first and foremost chosen seat of enterprise for the world's conversion," as one zealot wrote in the mid-1880s.[21] But for all to see, progress was bringing with it exactly the corruption that had long earlier been predicted.

Josiah Strong, a Protestant cleric and proselytizer much noted before and during the Gilded Age, enumerated all of America's ills and "perils" in a bestseller called *Our Country: Its Possible Future and Its Present Crisis*, published in 1885. There were immigration, Romanism (meaning Catholicism, an especially dreadful infection), Mormonism, intemperance, socialism, wealth, cities. All these brought America face to face with its gravest possible existential crisis:

> There are certain great focal points in history toward which the lines of past progress have converged, and from which have radiated the molding influences of the future. Such was the Incarnation, such was the German Reformation of the sixteenth century, and such are the closing years of the nineteenth century. They are one of the focal points of history, second in importance to that only which must always remain first; viz., the birth of Christ.[22]

This was the seventeenth century laid out in late-nineteenth-century nomenclature on the eve of the twentieth century. And for Strong and others of like and influential mind, there was only one way out of America's predicament. It was to settle the West, the frontier, where the slate was clean and virtue could still triumph over vice. But there was not much time. "It is proposed to show,"

Strong wrote as he began *Our Country*, "that the progress of Christ's kingdom in the world for centuries to come depends on the next few years in the United States."[23]

What was America, then? What had become of it and what was it to become? These are the questions that bore America to the doorstep of its century. The dilemma buried in them would define the decade during which the American century took its form. Could America go on as it had for its first hundred years? Was America to enter time and history at last, or would it hold fast to its claim of exemption from both? There were answers from many sides. This was the choice (then as now, one might add): a choice between history and myth.

————

Frederick Jackson Turner does not appear to have been an especially ambitious historian if we measure this by his productions. He finished but one work of note, a paper written for the American Historical Association in 1893. But Turner seems to have well understood the implications of "The Significance of the Frontier in American History" when he read the essay to the association three years later. Having grown up in the Middle West when the Middle West still displayed many of the features of "the West," Turner was, if anything, more personally concerned than many other scholars with America's transformation from a rural and agrarian society to one of cities and commerce, industry and immigrants. "The Turner thesis," as it is commonly known, was his reply. And its influence in years to come was matched only by the writer's commitment to the exceptionalist vision of America he advanced in it.

Turner wrote his thesis three years after the census bureau declared that the United States no longer had "a frontier line of settlement." Most scholars and many in government had understood this to be so roughly since the mid-1870s, but the official declaration of the disappearance of the frontier nonetheless seems to have weighed heavily upon Turner. We can but speculate as to whether he had read Josiah Strong—one doubts whether it would have mattered—but it was on the western frontier and nowhere else, he said, that Americans became American. It was there, Turner believed, that they acquired their indelible and exceptional individuality, the trait he thought marked them out more than any other from the rest of humanity.

Turner's argument turned on land and nature. The Atlantic seaboard, as he saw it, should be understood as nothing more than a westward extension of Europe. It was when Americans pushed further west still that they became something other than colonists whose frame of reference was the mother country:

> Thus the advance of the frontier has meant a steady movement away from the influence of Europe, a steady growth of independence on American lines. And to study this advance, the men who grew under these conditions, and the political, economic, and social results of it, is to study the really American part of our history.[24]

Americans, then, were made American by the unique experience of settling on virgin American soil. This thought gave Turner license to explore what it meant to be American in a way no one else had previously considered, and Turner took full flight with the room he had made for himself:

> This perennial rebirth, this fluidity of American life, this expansion westward with its new opportunities, its continuous touch with the simplicity of primitive society, furnish the forces dominating the American character. The true point

of view in the history of this nation is not the Atlantic coast, it is the Great West. . . . The frontier is the outer edge of the wave—the meeting point between savagery and civilization.

Turner delivered what was plainly an inspired performance. "The frontier is the line of the most rapid and effective Americanization," he said at one point. "A new order of Americanism rose" when settlers crossed the continent's great ranges. "In the crucible of the frontier the immigrants were Americanized, liberated, and fused into a mixed race, English in neither nationality nor characteristics."

These were forceful assertions when Turner made them to colleagues in 1896. The essay, indeed, figured prominently in the presidential election that year, which put McKinley, who enjoyed considerable backing from Wall Street and the East Coast political establishment, against William Jennings Bryan, a Nebraska native and a strenuous spokesman for the West and its farmers and miners. This is one reason the result of that election was lent so much weight at the time and in years to come. For a people already uncertain who they were and what defined their country, the victory of McKinley and Wall Street seemed to signal that the West no longer told America what it was. It would be useful as a source of myth and imagery—it would prove a trove in this respect—but the East and its money would determine what America was in what had just declared itself a new era.[25]

Turner's thesis no longer enjoys much credibility among historians. Even in the 1890s it was a monumental presupposition to assume that there was any such thing as an American character to talk about. Equally, to assert that unsettled land and exposure to "the simplicity of primitive society" were exclusively the formative factors in making Americans a unique people, and so markedly more individual than anyone else, was far too sweeping a generalization to last. We know now that much of what Turner rested his thesis upon, notably the question of frontier individuality (along with the ideology of individualism) stands on the very myth and popular imagery that the West was long to supply.

Nonetheless, Turner broke new ground with "The Significance of the Frontier." Among his most important contributions, he took no shelter in providential explanations of Americans and their fate. He was the first historian to attempt an account of the American continent's settlement in, as he put it himself, political, economic, and social terms—conditions on the ground. This is what the academy as a whole was attempting, one way or another, at the time: to preserve the case for American exceptionalism but to rest it atop rational and scientific explanations. It was a key transition in American intellectual history. In Turner's field, this alone would place him at the forefront of historians during what we now call the Progressive era.

But Turner's true importance as a theorist lies elsewhere. It is in what he suggested, or presaged. He made it plain in his essay that the closing of the frontier marked a turning point for the nation: "And now," he said in his final words, "four centuries from the discovery of America, at the end of a hundred years of life under the Constitution, the frontier has gone, and with its going has closed the first period of American history."

The *tristesse* in this closing remark is unmistakable. But Turner had already drawn a more important conclusion before he drew this one. With the closing of the "first period of American history" would open up the second, he all but stated in what must have been a moment or two earlier at the lectern in Boston:

He would be a rash prophet who should assert that the expansive character of American life has now entirely ceased.

Movement has been its dominant fact, and, unless this training has no effect upon a people, the American energy will
continually demand a wider field for its exercise.

This passage alone makes "The Significance of the Frontier"
worth dwelling upon. It also proves Turner to be a more prescient
thinker than he is ordinarily given credit for. It is impossible to know
the extent to which he understood the immense implications of this
passage. For in two simple sentences he defined the moment Americans then approached—the moment when they would commence
their era of overseas engagements and expansions. Had he followed
his own thought slightly farther, he would have defined the American century—notably in its first imperialist phase, which lay just
before him. Turner approved of it, as did his friend and scholarly
colleague Woodrow Wilson.

More than this, Turner described the essential character of an
era that was to last more than a hundred years. It would be rooted
in that culture of representation—the adumbrating of events and
their meanings by way of symbol and image—that Americans were
also about to enter fully upon. This was Turner's truly salient point,
though he did not use the phrase or address the matter directly. It
was the moment that all he thought of as going into the making
of Americans was passing into the past. Through the frame of representation, to put it another way, would America respond to the
coming of the modern. This frame could be re-presented again and
again. The slipping away of the nineteenth-century accounts, I think,
for Turner's elegiac tone. But the world beyond America's shores
would drive it and continually shape its "character" as once the continent's mountains and valleys and prairies had done. It was all to
be understood as more frontier: The world was our new wilderness.
"The really American part of our history" would go on. Two years

after Turner spoke in Boston, of course, it did by way of the war with Spain.

———

The *Maine,* the gleaming steamship that McKinley had dispatched to Havana harbor in January of 1898, became a cause célèbre when it exploded and sank a month later. With its hospital-white hull, state-of-the-art engines, and hydraulic gun turrets, it was a near-perfect expression of America as it wanted to represent itself to the world: of virtuous intent, technologically advanced, possessed of might, materially as capable as any other nation, if not more so.

But what was the *Maine* doing in Spanish waters? Equally, why would Dewey's Asiatic Squadron soon afterward sail into Manila Bay? These were the first manifestations of what Americans had come to call "the large policy," meaning the expansionist policy. What lay beneath the large policy?

Many motives have been advanced to explain America's great leap outward into the world beyond its shores. America had neglected its navy since the Civil War, and times had changed. Now the nation needed export markets for its wheat, corn, coal, and steel, and this required sea power to secure shipping lanes. It required coaling stations in faraway places. There was worrisome competition in the American hemisphere, notably from Britain and Germany. More broadly, America wanted a place among the imperial powers, especially in the Pacific. For many Americans, the national creed since the revolution still held: They would fight against all tyranny and for everyone living under it.

Historians have debated these motivations for many decades. Many now recognize that—to one degree or another—all of these national anxieties and aspirations informed the decision to challenge the Spanish empire. The Spanish were mistreating a restive population of Cubans, and Americans could not tolerate such cruelty on their southern doorstep: This was the argument advanced in the months before war was declared. But few writers have seen in the war with Spain an underlying choice—one made unconsciously but no less fatefully for that. This choice locates the cause of the war domestically, in the inner drives and fears of Americans. To put the point simply, the American choice in 1898 lay between democracy at home and empire abroad. Josiah Strong may have been merely an inspired Bible thumper, but he was oddly right about the singularity of the moment. To address its mounting difficulties at home—"the social problem," as it was commonly called—would have been to see the nation's place in worldly time and human history. It would have been to face the very different kind of country America was becoming and to imagine its democracy anew so as to address its new iniquities. The imperial project was thus an alternative, and one can easily say the less courageous, for it was at bottom a deflection, a flinch, a dereliction of the duties history had imposed. Americans, to put the point another way, still needed the wildernesses Turner had promised. TR would give them one. He represented the globalization of American exceptionalism—a large policy indeed. In effect, he would rest the American century on an eighteenth-century conception of the nation and its place in the world.

There was little bravery in the war with Spain, then—not if one reads it properly. To pursue it was to choose to prolong America's mythological idea of itself, just as Turner had predicted America would. It was to posit virtue—a version of virtue—against history. The Rough Riders and all who marched or sailed with them must have seemed at the time to represent a momentous new turn in America's destiny. How could they not? But beneath the mission and all the representation, paradoxically, lay an effort to avoid change, to stop history itself as it was perilously unfolding at home. There was no new turn, then. It was America's way out of the Gilded Age crisis. And so was the crisis of American exceptionalism resolved.

In 1901, while American troops were still fighting a legitimately democratic insurgency in the Philippines, Woodrow Wilson attempted to address the choice America had recently made. "Democracy and Efficiency" appeared in the *Atlantic Monthly* while Wilson was still a scholar at Princeton. He was a dozen years from the White House, but his essay is worth considering at length: It expresses some of the core contradictions that would define the American century. It is also an attempt to reconcile imperial exploits with an unsatisfactory democracy at home. And it suggests how a culture of representation would be embodied as a foreign policy. As such, it is as good a distillation as we have of early Wilsonian idealism, the encrypted code of the American century.

Wilson begins on a critical note—a historical note, indeed. Democracy in America had proven the success Tocqueville had foreseen, but it was in urgent need of repair. America had suddenly found itself a complex nation. "It is said that riots and disorder are more frequent amongst us than in any other country of the same degree of civilization," Wilson noted. "Justice is not always done in our courts; our institutions do not prevent, they do not seem even to moderate, contests between capital and labor." Summarizing his point about the quality of American democracy, Wilson wrote: "Our later life has disclosed serious flaws, has even seemed ominous of pitiful failure, in some of the things we most prided ourselves upon having managed well: notably in pure and efficient local government, in the successful organization of great cities, and in well-considered schemes of administration."[26]

Again there is the question, again the faint suggestion of agony: Was the virtuous republic crumbling before the eyes of Wilson's generation?

Farther on he elaborates:

We have supposed that there could be one way of efficiency for democratic governments, and another for monarchical. We have declined to provide ourselves with a professional civil service, because we deemed it undemocratic, we have made shift to do without a trained diplomatic and consular service, because we thought the training given by other governments to their foreign agents unnecessary in the case of affairs as simple and unsophisticated as the foreign relations of a democracy in politics and trade.

Such views were not unfamiliar by the time Wilson wrote: America needed a managerial class, a class of professionals and experts, for the old amateurism would not do in the new century. At the turn of the twentieth century, a new way of looking at the world was needed, and in America's case the need was pressing, for there was a palpable sense that the nation was floundering, unable to find itself in a new time:

A new era has come upon us like a sudden vision of things unprophesied, and for which no policy has been prepared. Here is straightaway a new frontage for the nations, this frontage toward the Orient. Our almost accidental possession of the Philippines has put us in the very presence of the forces which must make the politics of the twentieth century radically unlike the politics of the nineteenth. . . . They concern us as nearly as they concern any other nation of the world. They concern all nations for they shall determine the future of the race.

America needed a more equitable, effective, and efficient democracy if it was to become a world power: This was Wilson's explicit theme. The perfected republic must restore itself, and it was well within its powers to do so. But the true heart of Wilson's essay lay elsewhere. It had to do with how America conducted itself as an imperial power. America's government had succeeded because of its "suitability to the particular social, economic, and political conditions of the people and the country for whose use it had been framed." And it was this principle America must observe, having "awakened to our real relationship to the rest of mankind."

But here we find the critical fault line in Wilson's thinking. It was to run through the entire American century, defining America's conduct in one war or intervention after another. "The East is to be opened and transformed, whether we will or no," Wilson wrote. "The standards of the West are to be imposed upon it." And then:

> This we shall do, not by giving them out of hand our codes of political morality or our methods of political action, the generous gifts of complete individual liberty or the full-fangled institutions of American self-government . . . for these things are not blessings, but a curse, to undeveloped peoples, still in the childhood of their political growth; but by giving them, in the spirit of service, a government and rule which shall moralize them by being itself moral, elevate and steady them by being itself pure and steadfast, inducting them into the rudiments of justice and freedom. In other words, it is the aid of our character they need, and not the premature aid of our institutions. . . . We must aid their character and elevate their ideals, and then see what these will bring forth, generating after their kind.

Knowing all we know now, one must read these words today with an immense and sorrowful poignancy—an irony at the bottom of which lies a deep sadness rooted in one's consciousness of more than a century's worth of history, to say nothing of the world as we have it now. How was it Wilson could write in this fashion even as American soldiers were slaughtering Filipinos in a war that would drag on a dozen more years after Wilson wrote his essay? The question seems insoluble. Wilson was demonstrating that mythology would be essential if Americans were to explain themselves to themselves after 1898, so avoiding becoming merely another Atlantic power. Equally, it was Wilson who appeared to make possible the impossible thought that empire abroad and democracy at home were not mutually exclusive. And for a hundred years the nature of the American undertaking, precisely as Wilson described it, was not to change: It was not democracy Americans would aspire to transport around the globe—it was their democracy. This was to be the running theme of the imperial presidency as it has evolved—Wilson laying the first stones in the foundation.

It was, of course, a distinctive variety of imperialism Wilson put on offer: As others have observed, it was imperialism in the name of anti-imperialism.[27] In this respect "Democracy and Efficiency" was prescient. Unlike other imperial powers, Americans would not concern themselves overmuch with the export of any sort of political apparatus—legislative councils, civil servants, judges. Such things were mere machinery and could take care of themselves. It was our notion of the individual self that we would bestow upon our conquered—"the aid of our character." This was among the truly fateful distinctions that would make the American century American. In it lies far more hubris than mere colonization of the European kind. It explains, equally, why so much of the American century was violent and why success for a given people was so often achieved only in America's failure.

How much more insistent would the export of an idea of individuality and selfhood make America for the next hundred years—and how much more resistant the rest of the world? To impose one's idea of oneself upon another is an endless task, endless and infinite because impossible. But the attempt was necessary, nonetheless. It filled a deep need, something that lay far down in the American heart: the need to be accepted, even envied, as the crown of God's earthly creation. It answered the need to be understood as exceptional. If people exposed to Americans did not become like Americans—or, worse, had no desire to do so—what of the American project, the American century being its fulfillment? The suggestion would have to be that the mission as Americans conceived of it was either a mistake or a fraud. The myths were merely myths. How readily would any society accept such a thought? History is filled with people who accepted decline, or even extinction, rather than surrender their accumulation of stories. However one reads these passages, they capture one of the tragedies of the American century: the nation's inability, as it sought its new "Wests," to leave others to themselves—even as it proclaimed precisely such as its intent.

———

"America created the twentieth century," Gertrude Stein wrote in *The Autobiography of Alice B. Toklas,* "and since all the other countries are now either living or commencing to be living a twentieth-century life, America having begun the creation of the twentieth century in the sixties of the nineteenth century is now the oldest country in the world."[28]

Stein published the *Autobiography* in 1933. And by that time America may well have seemed the most modern of all nations—

and hence the oldest, as Stein put it. Certainly she was right to identify America closely with the unfolding of the twentieth century nearly a decade before Henry Luce gave it its name. The relationship between America and the twentieth century's course was to be intimate.

But Stein's clever *mot* does not hold on close consideration. It is time and history that make nations, not the other way around. America's claim to stand outside of both grew ever more insistent as the twentieth century proceeded. But this was because it was less and less defensible in fact. Even a brief gloss of the Spanish-American War reveals plainly enough that the march of events led America into it, however eagerly it went. To assert that any nation created a given time is to assert that nation's exceptionalism. Consciously or otherwise, this is what Stein meant to say as to America and its century and which created which. It was well dressed in her Modernist language, but Stein's thought was perfectly conventional.

There is equally the matter of the modern. It is ordinary enough to take material advances and scientific accomplishments as the measure of a nation's modernity. But are these truly what make a nation modern? The condition of modernity derives from a nation's consciousness of itself in time: It is aware of where it stands by way of its past and its future. It does not live any longer according to mythologies. To be modern, then, one must think historically. Many are the cultures, societies, and nations that have advanced far on the material plane but remain premodern in their thinking, their awareness of themselves.

This was the American condition as it opened the American century: accomplished in its material culture and its sciences, but still living in a pre-historicist consciousness. Modernism emerged in Europe as a response to history's heavy weight. But America felt no such weight, and so one can ask, What need had it for the modern?

"Every man now knows that the world is to be changed,—changed according to an ordering of Providence hardly so much as foreshadowed until it came."[29] That is Woodrow Wilson again, in the essay previously examined. And it is a truer account of America's relationship with its time than Stein's. America was old as it entered the twentieth century, but not as Stein reckoned it. America was old because it was almost singularly premodern at the twentieth century's turn—in its precepts, its beliefs, and its assumptions.

America's presence and influence were to grow by magnitudes in the decades that followed the war with Spain. By 1945 it was indisputably the planet's most powerful nation. But how did it understand this power? Was it as modern in its outlook as all the science it had put into World War II suggested? Had it yet to learn to think historically? Or did the re-representation of old myths still drive it on, ever in need of new frontiers?

COLD WAR MAN

—

We are the poorer for the global responsibilities which we bear. And the fulfillments of our desires are mixed with frustrations and vexations.
—Reinhold Niebuhr, *The Irony of American History*, 1952

Later on in his life, after all the fame and sorrow and controversy had come to him, Charles Lindbergh recalled his first flight in an airplane. It was April 9, 1922, and Lindbergh was a passenger in a two-seat biplane flying above the cornfields of Nebraska.

"Trees became bushes, barns toys," Lindbergh recalled three decades later. "Cows turned into rabbits as we climbed. I lose all conscious connection with the past. I live only in the moment in this strange, unmortal place, crowded with beauty, pierced with danger."[1]

The transporting power of machines was much on people's minds in the 1920s. But not everyone greeted it with Lindbergh's innocent delight. A few years after Lindbergh flew, a French writer named

Paul Morand published a brief, curious book called *De la vitesse,* which translates roughly as *On Speed.* "There is in speed something irresistible and forbidding," Morand began, "a tragic beauty of indescribable consequence, a necessity and a curse." So did Morand open the relentlessly cold eye he would cast on science and machines and the speed they put at humankind's disposal. He reserved a special critique for America: "The world's fastest nation," he called it.[2]

Later on Morand writes as if he were addressing Lindbergh directly. "Which is it—are we lost in speed and therefore to history, or are we lost to history and therefore escape into speed?" he asks. "Speed annihilates place—speed kills form. . . . Speed inhabits the spirit by an infinite succession of images."

As to America, it was guilty of *un délit de fuite,* a crime of avoidance. "The Americans are very close to believing that speed equals beauty, truth, well-being," Morand asserts. "One begins to perceive—and psychoanalysis is not a stranger to this discovery—that if an entire continent is thus the victim of speed, it pursues, more than money, speed in itself as a means of not thinking and avoiding certain painful, unconscious problems and hidden complexes."

Morand concludes with this: "Sometimes I've had the impression of a civilization not moving toward progress but in flight before its specters."

The striking feature of these two men's perceptions is their similarity. One would think this unlikely: Lindbergh was a college dropout from the Midwest, Morand a sophisticated diplomat and writer with a complex political life in Paris (and later Vichy). Yet they both understood that beauty and danger were inseparable in the machines man made and that speed provided a kind of illusory means of escape from the ordinary human condition. They both recognized that machines had the power to deliver man from the past and confine him in an eternal present. The difference between the two men was but one: The American loved the inducements and seductions of machines and speed, while the other, the European, found in them a source of infinite dread.

———

Lindbergh and Morand lived during the period when science was at last making its way into ordinary life. After the uncertainties of Modernism and the disaster of World War I, science offered a route to the predictable, a path to order amid immense historical flux. And the natural and physical sciences themselves—biology, physics, chemistry—became the models upon which other sciences, specifically the social sciences, developed. But science was also something else: It was in part a recoil from a world wherein old meanings had been lost. All of the new, evolving sciences had, then, a certain element of fear submerged in them. Science is humankind's way of exploring the natural world and its inhabitants—a thrusting forward. But buried in it, we so often find, is a dread of the unknown and a compulsion to conquer it by knowing it in its every aspect. Science and fear: They are far from strangers.

There is, therefore, a relationship between science and security that must not be missed. For Americans, science was to become a source of collective self-confidence. Few understood this better in the 1920s than John Dewey, the noted American pragmatist. In 1929, the year Paul Morand was critiquing speed, science, and America's taste for both, Dewey published *The Quest for Certainty*, a vigorous defense of the scientific "arts." To make use of these arts was how humankind acted upon the universe. "It is a commentary on the slight control man has achieved over himself by means of control over nature, that the method of action has been felt to manifest dangerous pride, even defiance of the powers that be," Dewey wrote. "The souls who have predicted that by means of the arts man might establish a kingdom of order, justice, and beauty through mastery of nature's energies and laws have been few and little heeded."[3]

Humankind, in other words, had been unduly shy of science, as if it were among the black arts—a transgressive pursuit. Dewey was one of those predicting souls who thought otherwise. His book posited the immense value to be derived from scientific inquiry at a time when science and the devices it produced had left many flummoxed and many others critical. It was in part an attack on established distinctions between knowledge (the ideal) and action (the realized)—truth and method, in other words. Dewey was especially bold on this point. "Barring the fears which war leaves in its train," he wrote, "it is perhaps a safe speculation that if contemporary western man were completely deprived of all his old beliefs about knowledge and action he would assume, with a fair degree of confidence, that it is within his power to achieve a reasonable degree of security in life."[4]

Dewey was not alone in contemplating the question of security in a modern, scientific context. Late in 1914, a group of influential New Yorkers led by a corporate lawyer named S. Stanwood Menken had organized something called the National Security League. The league was an announcement of its time and of the time to come, and it favored an altogether different notion of security. In *The Quest for Certainty* Dewey had urged Americans to seek security amid the uncertainty and change that come with historical time. In this, Dewey had a modern mind. But his was remote, indeed, from the National Security League's thinking. In its view, there was no place for any such flux. A fear of change, always present in the American psyche, would perversely turn Dewey's "quest" into something near to a cult. Certainty would derive from the creation of a world that, by way of science and machines, was to be altogether fixed according to human desires.[5]

The National Security League, which remained active into the 1940s, was an early manifestation of an impulse among Americans that would eventually lead to the national security state as we now know it. Its concern was "preparedness," a twentieth-century version of an argument that extended back to Hamilton. Decades before Joseph McCarthy, it wanted to ensure "100 per cent Americanism" across the nation by stifling all dissent; in 1918 it urged America's first modern witch-hunt. In the league's view, security derived only from power. In time, this idea of security would produce immense new defense and intelligence establishments—opaque, much dependent upon secrecy and distance from the electorate. Fear would be transformed from an individual emotion into a social condition. It would become normative, and it would invest all who lived with it in the success of the American mission. Judgments rooted in fear were to be accepted as rational judgments. This was the destiny of Dewey's "quest for certainty." Again perversely, the national security state would produce among Americans a permanent condition of insecurity. Dewey could not have foreseen this, for the proximity of science, technology, and speed to the production and reproduction of fear was not yet evident.

The world I describe is, of course, well with us now. It is the world, one senses, that Paul Morand managed to intuit but no more, for it was then in a formative stage. These are the roots of the Cold War world, which came into being a mere decade and a half after Dewey and Morand wrote. And among its most essential characteristics we can count a new kind of power, greatly expanded government prerogative, and the heightened national preoccupation with certainty that had first suggested itself at the century's start. Certainty in its cultish iteration would become an obsession. Nothing would be deemed impossible, and there was nowhere in the universe Americans could not go to achieve it.

No period of American history can be counted so extreme in its assumptions as the Cold War decades—the assumption of moral superiority, the assumption of right and prerogative beyond law, the assumption of divine dispensation. No period matches it for its resort to the foundational myths—notably the utopian idea of a world made over in the American image—to explain itself. Except possibly for the revolutionary era, in no other time was the American combination of confidence and apprehension on such full display. We come to one of the American century's paradoxes: The more power a nation accumulates, the less secure does it feel itself to be, the less is certainty within its grasp.

———

Americans were slightly unsteady after the victories of April and August of 1945. Personal accounts from that time give an impression not unlike that of 1898: Americans had reached for something and were a little unnerved to realize the enormity of the prize when they had it at last. In a matter of months America found itself incontestably the world's most powerful nation. What should it do? The question was especially pressing when it came to Europe, Stalin, and the Soviet Union. Roosevelt had planned for a relationship based on mutual cooperation. But Roosevelt's vision did not long survive his passing. The days of "Uncle Joe" were over by 1946, as a new sensibility, arrogant and insecure all at once, took hold in Washington. What should America do in this new mood?

This ambivalence lingered long, at least among ordinary Americans. As late as 1947, when the Truman administration was planning to intervene in Greece to defend a crumbling monarchy against a popular insurgency of numerous hues, it was not clear whether Americans would accept this, the opening incident of the Cold War. Dean Acheson, Truman's undersecretary of state at the time, was perfectly clear on the matter. "It is a question of whether two-thirds of the area of the world is to be controlled by Communists," he said as he contemplated Greece, the Mediterranean, and the lands beyond.[6] But how to present this to Congress and the public was delicate: Neither was in the mood for anything that might resemble or provoke conflict.

The administration debated internally for many days before what would soon be known as the Truman Doctrine was finally delivered in Congress on March 12, 1947. The announced object of the exercise was to defend democracy and freedom in Europe, even if Greeks enjoyed neither under George II and subsequently Paul I, George's neofascist brother. The true purpose of the Greek intervention was the assertion of American power in American interests against a certain (quite inaccurate) reassessment of Moscow's intentions. In the Greek case Washington's concern extended to the protection of Middle Eastern oil supplies. Whether an American leader could say all this to a public still breathing the air of postwar idealism was the subject of much discussion within the administration that winter. At the start of this period, the State Department drafted a request for aid, handed it to the Greek chargé d'affaires, and asked to have it signed and delivered back from Athens to Washington as soon as possible. That would help win congressional and public hearts and minds, Acheson and others reckoned. But should the Soviets be mentioned in Truman's address? The true nature of the monarchy and its adversaries? What about the United Nations? "It was still not possible," a State Department official later recalled, "to tell the American people what the real issue was."[7] This remarkable observation portended much. Some of the most important secrets Americans were to keep during the Cold War were the ones they kept from themselves.

In the end, Truman left the Soviets out of it, at least explicitly, and spoke only of alternative ways of life when he went to Congress to request $400 million in economic and military assistance for the Greeks. "I believe that it must be the policy of the United States to support free peoples who are resisting attempted subjugation by armed minorities or by outside pressures," Truman concluded. "I believe that we must assist free peoples to work out their own destinies in their own way."[8] With those words, as perverse under the circumstances as Wilson's had been half a century earlier, America began to redefine what it meant to be a world power. No one had ever before asserted so sweeping an authority; privilege and immunity were to be a kind of demotic form of exceptionalism. What America became on the basis of Truman's commitment would be like nothing the world had ever before seen.

In Greece, Washington began nothing less than the Americanization of internationalism—as, decades later, globalization would implicitly mean Americanization. Wilsonianism would lose all trace of ideals, making neo-Wilsonianism not much more than an empty narrative Americans could read back to themselves. Wilson's idealism had initially been predicated on an eighteenth-century thought, the utopian assumption that the world looked forward to greeting Americans with optimistic smiles. Now this gave way to a policy rooted in fear and power. The greater the uncertainty, it has been said, the greater the resort to ideology, and from the Greek intervention onward American policy would take on an ever more evident ideological coloring. In the end, Americans would do much to create the very world they thought they wanted to avert—disorderly, often deadly, opaque, confused, incessantly anxious. In Greece, Washington had its first corrupt, reactionary, and violent client, and the Pax Americana had begun. Wherever on the planet "freedom" was threatened, so was American security.

When was it that Americans began to place more faith in science—science and the power deriving from it—than in democracy? The question is key because the elevation of science was so essential in creating what I am calling Cold War man. It was science and machinery that won World War II, and the lesson was not lost among the victors. It would be difficult to overstate the extent to which scientific progress altered humanity's relations with the world in the years afterward. This was when Americans began to discover that in science lay security—or at least a seductive illusion of it. Once the thought took hold, it is remarkable how expendable democracy would at times become.

The best one can do is go back to the beginning, to the Spanish war and the *Maine:* From the century's start it was science America was eager to put before the world—material achievement—more than democracy. This is a simple judgment based on the historical record and the recognitions of some of the period's better minds. "It is my belief that science is to wreck us," Henry Adams wrote but four years later, "and that we are like monkeys monkeying with a loaded shell; we don't in the least know or care where our practically infinite energies come from or will bring us to."[9]

But as with so much of what Adams wrote, his was a minority view. Consider this flight of exceptionalist faith by a prominent scientist named Rexford G. Tugwell. He wrote in the mid-twenties:

Our civilization ... may slip and regress, falling into the mad desuetude of ruin that overtook Assyria and Egypt, Greece and Rome ... fall from the tree of time and rot like a withered leaf in the mold of common earth. There is that chance. But alternatively we may think of ourselves in a different metaphor, not a leaf on the tree of time but as an historical force, with power over time, over space, over mankind itself. We may master our fate.[10]

There is a whiff of the Cold War in this passage—its hubris, its sense of science as a limitless endeavor. The Cold War would elevate science to an almost sacred status among Americans, but as the effusive Tugwell makes plain, this was not a sudden rise to preeminence. It had been cultivated over many years. The mastery of time, space, humanity, fate itself: Science, by the time Tugwell wrote, had already begun to emerge as an instrument of mythological fulfillment. This was the result of a transformation that has lasted until the present day. It occurred in stages.

Science in nineteenth-century America was an unsystematic enterprise. The paradigm was the tinkering inventor in his homemade laboratory. Out of such men and such places came the light bulb, the Wright brothers' airplane, Ford's car, countless patented medicines of greater or lesser worth, and so on. But by the second decade of the twentieth century, this phase of scientific development was giving way. In its place came science funded by a few wealthy corporations and a few new philanthropic organizations such as the Carnegie Institution and the Rockefeller Foundation.

This changed the face and workings of science fundamentally. Universities such as Princeton, Stanford, MIT, Chicago, and Harvard became the recipients not only of corporate beneficence but also of corporate culture. Wealthy sponsors would not only fund specific projects; they also would encourage the management practices that had produced their wealth. This was the beginning of what would become "Big Science." Scientists were to be something like science executives or managers. They contracted for projects and submitted progress reports. Peer reviews in the standard academic fashion came to resemble corporate board meetings.

Most important, the very purpose of science, the reason Americans would pursue it so avidly, began to change just as fundamentally. Until the early decades of the twentieth century, the aims of science were exploration and discovery. Reflecting the interests of science's new benefactors and the early signs of the cult of certainty, these purposes started to give way to a focus on control. Dewey hinted at this shift; so, in its way, did the National Security League. It would be difficult to overstate its importance, notably during and after World War II. Exploration and discovery can be considered pure pursuits. Control is otherwise. No longer an endeavor to discern and observe the natural world, science becomes humanity's assertion of itself into nature—a very different thing. Its ultimate object could be no other than the humanization of the universe. And as I have already suggested, with control as its goal science begins to intersect rather impurely with democracy and politics.

Big Science would eventually alter not just the physical sciences but mathematics, economics, and the social sciences as well. The social sciences, in particular, would divorce themselves from historical analysis in the early twentieth century. They would be sterilized, we might say. This produced both a bureaucratization in the sciences and what we call "scientism," meaning the belief in the scientific method as the source of solutions to all problems. Instead of historical or psychological perspective, the social sciences sought to make themselves "objective" and "value free." And the absence of history— an absence that has marked off American social sciences from Europe's ever since—would allow American social scientists to serve the exceptionalist mission.

All of the sciences would become more abstract in this period, more given to statistical analysis, more technocratic, more prone to theorizing the individual as a being as predictable as a machine, and altogether more devoted to the concerns, first, of corporate America and, latterly, the armed forces: the control of production, the control of managers, the control of markets, the control of equipment, the control of consumers, the control of troops and ordnance. Fatefully, these new objectives began to break down barriers between disciplines, such that physicists were suddenly talking to economists and sociologists to mathematicians. The influence of physics would prove especially important in the emergence of the Chicago School of free-market economics in the late 1940s.

World War II marked a new phase in the history of science and for those who practiced it. The military was now the primary benefactor, and its needs were similar to what had been before in some cases, different in others. The most famous device to emerge from wartime scientific research was the computer, though one might also mention radar and the atomic bomb. But apart from weapons systems, the military wanted scientists to work on various aspects of communications, control, intelligence, systems analysis, operations research, and other rudiments of the high-technology military we know today. These fields and others like them would dominate scientific thinking for many decades. Such questionable pursuits as "game theory" and "rational choice theory" arose from this environment. Science and scientists and the institutions where they worked were, fair to say, becoming well-rewarded captives of the armed forces.

———

The man who conceived of, created, and managed wartime science was named Vannevar Bush. Bush did not act alone, it should be noted at the outset, but if America had a wartime science czar it was Vannevar Bush. Bush had begun his career in electrical engineering at MIT, taught at Tufts, and had been head of research at the defense contractor later to be known as Raytheon. He was engaged in secret research for the navy as early as the 1930s; in 1937 he was named president of the Carnegie Institution.[11]

This background put Bush in a position to approach President Roosevelt in 1940 with the idea of creating a National Defense Research Committee, the first organization of its kind in the American government. This was one early point of departure in the construction of the national security state. Bush used the committee to reproduce the working model he had grown accustomed to. There would be comparatively little support for government laboratories; instead, government funds would flow to university and industrial laboratories to underwrite weapons development programs and a variety of other defense-related projects. The departure is key: This would be how the American economy, American society, and American universities and corporations would gradually be militarized.

In mid-1941, with war hard upon the United States, FDR created the Office for Scientific Research and Development. Bush became its head. The OSRD had a broader mandate than the research committee: It could fund weapons production as well as research. And in it Bush's model crystallized: More than ninety percent of the OSRD's funds went to nine elite universities. It oversaw a vast expanse of military-related scientific research—research that required ever more collaboration across disciplinary lines. In effect, Bush had already put in place the model for Cold War science management.

In November 1944, Roosevelt asked Bush to submit a report on the management of science once the war had ended. FDR did not live to see *Science—The Endless Frontier*. Bush submitted it in July 1945, a few months after Roosevelt's death put Truman in the White House.[12]

Bush's thesis reflected much of his own experience. To be fair, he did not dwell exclusively upon military-related research, but he was unsparing in the attention he paid to it. "There must be more—

and more adequate—military research in peacetime," Bush wrote. "It is essential that the civilian scientists continue in peacetime some portion of those contributions to national security which they have made so effectively during the war. This can best be done through a civilian-controlled organization with close liaison with the Army and Navy but with funds direct from Congress, and the clear power to institute military research which will supplement and strengthen that carried on directly under the control of the Army and Navy."[13]

In so many words, Bush was advocating for the national security state and arguing against any thought of dismantling the sprawling wartime scientific research apparatus that had been built up under his direction. Presumably to cultivate popular support for Bush's version of Big Science, the Truman administration decided to make *Science—The Endless Frontier* public. Almost overnight Bush found himself a famous American. And among the interesting things about his report is the way he cast scientists and science for American consumption. "The pioneer spirit is still vigorous within the Nation," he noted in his covering letter. "Science offers a largely unexplored hinterland for the pioneer who has the tools for the task."[14]

Bush was writing in the obligatory American code. In the report itself we are given this:

> It has been basic United States policy that Government should foster the opening of new frontiers. It opened the seas to clipper ships and furnished land for pioneers. Although those frontiers have more or less disappeared, the frontier of science remains. It is in keeping with the American tradition—one which has made the United States great—that new frontiers shall be made accessible for development by all American citizens.[15]

Bush's model worked straight to plan in the immediate postwar years. Federal spending on research and development came to about $1 billion in the 1949–50 fiscal year, and ninety percent of it was defense related; ninety-six percent of university research funding came from the military. During the Korean War, two-thirds of American scientists and engineers were engaged in defense-related work. Over time, McCarthyist intrusions took their toll on this free-flowing arrangement, much to Bush's chagrin. But then came the Soviets' launch of *Sputnik* in 1957. By that time, there was no going back on America's investment in science as a source of self-confidence. This can be measured by the shock the Soviets administered when they sent *Sputnik* into space, and also by the swell of national pride that accompanied Alan Shepard's brief ascent three years later. In effect, *Sputnik* pushed what already amounted to a military-scientific-industrial complex into a kind of new golden age.

By the early 1960s, it was clear that the Bush model was the foundation of a relationship among government, corporate power, and science that had no antecedent in American history. When Eisenhower delivered his famous "military-industrial complex" speech as he left office in January 1961, it is true that he introduced a new term into the American vocabulary. But he did not, we now know, offer Americans a forecast or a warning: He was announcing what had already been accomplished.[16] We still live with this concatenation of power—an incessantly consolidated version of it. In an executive order issued in March 2012, the White House gave administration and department officials the duty to monitor the civilian economy "to improve the international competitiveness of specific domestic industries and their abilities to meet national defense program needs." With this comes the authority to implement national planning and to take control of "industrial facilities owned by private persons."

This is a Cold War legacy. So far as I know this executive order—one among numerous like it—went unreported in the press.[17]

———

Vannevar Bush had done his job, plainly enough. And he got it done in the name of a new American frontier. There could hardly be a clearer example of the continuity of myth and ideology in American history. Anyone alive during the years just glossed will recall the incessant reiteration of this motif. It is one key to the psychological makeup of Cold War man. What, after all, does any frontier invoke in any of us if not a heightened anticipation of discovery along with a gripping fear of the unknown? Science was not the only frontier during the Cold War, we must remember. Since the Truman Doctrine—which amounted to a radical reinterpretation of Wilsonianism—the globe itself and all that went on in it was America's frontier, too. But the one would serve the other: Science would see us through the universal struggle with the Soviets, just as it had seen us through World War II, even if America would consistently act more out of apprehension than confidence.

Images of the frontier are but one form of a nostalgia characteristic of the Cold War years. There were others, each evoking (as nostalgia always does) a cleansed past, a simplified past, and above all an innocent past. One was a longing for the world as it once had been: the long nineteenth-century peace that preceded the war with Spain. In the American consciousness, that period lingered as the way life naturally was, and the contested twentieth century was all about recovery and restoration. The project was one of a return to a pastoral time gone by, if only by way of image and representation. This is why Wilsonianism had been understood at first to be a temporary necessity.

World War II was another object of national nostalgia, for it was abruptly remote. Pushing the German bombings and the atomic attacks on Hiroshima and Nagasaki into the space of a forgotten background—no easy task—Americans could look upon the war as a clean, untarnished defense of liberty and democracy. They could have heroes. It was the last time they could make any claim to being both powerful and innocent: The two in combination would never be America's again, not even by way of illusion. From its very onset, the Cold War was more complex in its character and its morality. It created a new kind of time such that the temporality of events was erased. The past could be understood in terms of time, but Cold War time was suspended, as if in a chemical solution, in an eternal and unchanging present. With all its strategy and technology and geopolitical maneuvering, the Cold War swiftly pushed World War II into a kind of deep, inaccessible past. It became a story, for Americans needed one of simple victory as the Cold War's uncertainties and ambiguities grew evident. The war was not the midcentury mark one might expect so much as a final act in the great "back there" of the century's early decades.

Who, then, was Cold War man? The question is answered as much according to what was made of him as to what he chose to make of himself, for Cold War man was a construction to a far greater extent than most people alive during those years have ever realized. He is worthy of scrutiny, for he was something new in America. He was a disturbing figure, inflexible in his thinking, suited for one way of life and no other, cut off from his past—and altogether necessary for his time: The Cold War could not have been waged without him.

The attribute that comes immediately to mind is the childlike manner in which he allowed the Cold War world to envelop him. There was no seeing out of the Cold War universe, and this deprived Cold War man of any fulsome understanding of it—a condition remaining with us. He was an innocent at home, in other words. And this accounts for many of the traits we now associate with this generation of Americans. He was forgetful of or indifferent to much that was done in his name. He was mesmerized by Paul Morand's "infinite succession of images," now made incessantly available by way of film and television—displays of speed, of scientific capability, of power, of fear. There was his extreme conformity and his commitment to the cult of certainty. And in the greatest of nations, Cold War man submitted to what I will call the tyranny of American happiness. Happiness had been a Western obsession since the eighteenth century—"the Grail of the modern world," as one good scholar put it.[18] Numerous prominent and lesser authors—Samuel Johnson and Voltaire among them—celebrated the quest for and achievement of happiness. Happiness was taken as a sign of virtue, and it was conceived of as a new moral duty. This was felt especially in America, for what was America if not "Heaven now on earth"? One could hardly be American and announce a state of unhappiness. And so did happiness become essential to Americans again a couple of centuries later, for it would prove them moral and prove them right. The Cold War was fought partly with images—enviable American smiles prominent among them. This tedious preoccupation with a hollow variety of happiness accounts, at least in part, for the infantilization of American culture even as the nation's behavior turned lethal in so many places overseas.

Cold War man prompts questions. He seems distant, but how much of ourselves do we find in him when we look back upon his time? C. Wright Mills, the noted sociologist, warned as early as 1956 that a new technocratic elite made of political figures, chief executives, scientists, and generals had consolidated itself, rendering America "more a formal political democracy than a democratic social structure."[19] What had the twentieth century unleashed such that so many Americans could live in a state of anchorless drift? Why was Cold War man so susceptible to manipulation, so vulnerable to manifestations of authority, so easily deluded?

In each case, it comes to the persistence of myths within the structure of American beliefs. Myth sustained Americans in the face of an ever more disorderly world. It kept them from facing what they had made of themselves by way of the Cold War—or what had been made of them. At home, myth left Americans with no conception of their institutions as historical (and therefore in need of attention). In consequence, they were quite ready to accept the vision of human society then fashionable among conservative intellectuals: The ideological phase of human history had ended. Liberal capitalism in its American manifestation constituted humankind's highest achievement, and there was no logical alternative to it—and no need for an alternative. This is where his myths led Cold War man at midcentury.

Mythical thinking magnifies fear. So often myths foretell clarifying cataclysms, making what is at stake larger than life itself. Fear, naturally enough, grows large, too. It envelops the personality. The atomic detonations in 1945 are essential to understanding this tendency toward fearfulness during the Cold War. They amplified it exponentially. Fear became sociological; one could not see beyond fear. It was in this environment that scientists made the supremacy of science and technology a grounded belief among Americans. At Hiroshima and Nagasaki, and in numerous other contexts, science had founded a universal climate of fear. But no one could imagine a solution to this weight of dread and terror other than the pursuit of more science, more technology, and more speed—the last being the cause of a profound alienation of humanity from its surroundings.

Like the scientific community itself, Americans began to entertain the impulse to control taken to its farthest extreme. The overweening aspiration of Dr. Tugwell during the 1920s—time, space, and fate could all be ours to control—only deepened during the Cold War. But the Cold War years brought Americans up against a problem that had been waiting to be discovered and understood at least since Henry Adams's day and the subsequent rise of scientism. Many of the nation's brightest minds were scientific minds, yet they seemed to have given little thought to what science was for, to possess little grasp of society, and to suffer a fulsome confusion, in their fascination with the scientific, between means and ends. This was scientism—as I have said, science sterilized. From this perspective, there was little that was heroic in America's management of science during the Cold War. Onward from Trinity Site in the New Mexican desert, where the first atomic explosion was set off, science has repeatedly shown us our capacity to dedicate rational processes to irrational ends.

At its extreme, science became an instrument of rebellion—a revolt against the human condition itself because of the uncertainties and limitations implicit in it. In this respect, it was something of exceptional importance to Americans: It was their midcentury response to history's knock on the door. Hannah Arendt wrote in 1958 of the extent scientists had begun to "act into nature":

> This started harmlessly enough with the experiment in which men were no longer content to observe, to register, and contemplate whatever nature was willing to yield in her own appearance, but began to prescribe conditions and to provoke natural processes. What then developed into an ever-increasing skill in unchaining elemental processes, which, without the interference of men, would have lain dormant and perhaps never have come to pass, has finally ended in a veritable act of "making" nature, that is, of creating "natural" processes which without men would never exist and which earthly nature by herself seems incapable of accomplishing.[20]

Dewey, in his praise of science back in 1929, could not have foreseen America's Faustian aspirations at World War II's end, any more than he could have foreseen the Cold War. But the desire literally to conquer nature by making machines that would contend with it and, indeed, triumph over it was an essential feature of Cold War man. The craving, above all others, was for the feeling of certainty. Jean-Pierre Dupuy, a historian of science, calls the result "the mechanization of the mind."[21] In the American case, I prefer the militarization of the mind, for there was in this country ever less space between science and its military application. It could be no other way, given how thoroughly American thinking was framed by the military and its Cold War. In time, the military began to impinge on the logic of daily life—to make itself a palpable presence. It was overinfluential in American universities and the source of too many millions of jobs, artfully distributed through almost every congressional district. One of the early conduits in the psychological transformation I describe was the Federal Civil Defense Administration, founded in 1951 to develop "bomb consciousness" and help American families learn to live through a nuclear attack. It would be difficult to imagine a more effective way to transmit official thinking, scientific postulation, and military regimentation downward to ordinary Americans. In extreme cases—and I recall seeing a couple—the family began to take on characteristics of a paramilitary unit.[22]

American scientists were not indifferent to the impact of their work. Neoliberal economics, in essence a Cold War faith, emerged from their interdisciplinary collaborations, and complete control—in this case over the individual's behavior—was again the object. In time, the citizen would be reduced to a consumer and the consumer to a machine that responds with perfect predictability to the input of any given set of data as supplied by the market. There was also a political dimension to this pencil portrait. Science came to contend with democracy because the latter, while it was a process, did not always yield the desired result. There was a current of thinking within the scientific and scholarly communities that supported this manner of measuring the one against the other. Many noted intellectuals—Hans Morgenthau and Friedrich von Hayek prominent among them—had watched the Weimar Republic collapse into the Nazi era or the sweep of Soviet-modeled socialism across what quickly became the Eastern bloc. In consequence, they entertained considerable animosity toward democracy and its institutions (notably elections). The political process, they argued, cannot be left to ordinary men and women: Only a technocratic elite, properly trained to stand at the intersection of science, the military, industry, politics, and ideology, would be qualified to safeguard it.[23]

These threads of thinking help explain more features of Cold War man—things he did or did not do or simply accepted as others did them. The false equation of science and democracy was especially pernicious: It led to a nearly comprehensive loss of all transcendent values among Americans. But other traits, attributes, and tendencies also appeared. Most Americans failed entirely to register Arendt's observation that the greater humankind's technological mastery of nature, the less can we manage the consequences of what we do. No thorough account of the decline of democracy during the McCarthyist years can fail to disturb the reader not old enough to remember it directly. Equally, one must account for the tolerance many Americans displayed as the national security state was built and for the coups, assassinations, and other interventions abroad that it conducted—with or without Americans' knowledge. Who was Cold War man to acquiesce in silence as such operations were executed? Alternatively, who was he to accept such a degree of ignorance as to what was done in his name? This silence and this ignorance should be considered and understood. They reflect an undesirable, ultimately destructive relationship with power—detectable here and there all through history but a notable tragedy when placed against America's founding purpose. Given that many of the American century's interventions were directed toward aspiring democratic movements and legitimately elected political figures and governments, one is forced to conclude that America during the Cold War did at least as much damage to democracy around the world as it did to the communist cause. This is a reality—one of many—that Americans have yet to face. The mark of Cold War man's silence remains deeply upon us.

This brings us to Wilson's famous assertion when he addressed Congress in 1917. "The world must be made safe for democracy" was what he said. Henry Steele Commager, one of the great historians of his generation, was among many liberals who believed that the Cold War disrupted America's democratic project: It was the perversion of an ideal.[24] I do not accept this. The Cold War simply magnified the true project—to make the world safe for American democracy and the American "character," to take Wilson's term—into a global mission. This is why America got the independence and decolonization era that followed World War II—among the most important interims in twentieth-century history—so badly wrong. America could have had a thousand friends, but it ended with few, and even those few finished up questioning it. America could not understand democracies unless they were in its own image.

With danger more or less everywhere, danger even where there was none, the Cold War made fear a permanent force of the American century. This was postwar America; given the nation's sentiments and choices, it could not have been otherwise. At the moment it achieved its greatest power, we find a new variant of what had haunted Americans from the first—now an infinite, abstract fear, in its prevalence a uniquely modern kind of fear. The objective correlatives arrived in 1949, when the Soviets exploded their first bomb and Mao took Beijing. These events shook Americans to the core of their assumptions and beliefs. They also evoked a fear of failure, and this last arose directly from American myth. "It is abundantly clear," Commager wrote in 1968, "that the myth of uniqueness carried with it, and all but required, the myth of superiority."[25] The Cold War, then, had to prove out centuries of American belief if Americans were to go on being Americans in the way they commonly took to be their destiny. Fear was the idiom in which Cold War man spoke. And it induced an incessant dedication to vigilance—another attribute of Cold War man we have yet to reckon with.

This held true at home as well as abroad. For as much as anything else, Cold War man came to live in a context I will call the sayable and the unsayable. This began quite early. Eleven days after Truman addressed Congress on the Greek question, he created the Federal Employee Loyalty and Security Program, so beginning the Cold War at home. Rather large portions of political, social, and economic discourse were thereafter understood to be out of bounds. Anyone alive then will recall the unwritten rules. What was acceptable in social contexts, what could be written in newspapers and books, what could be shown in Hollywood films, what teachers could teach and scholars think, what a political figure could and could not say if he or she wanted election—all of this was circumscribed by way of a kind of silent censorship in which most Americans acquiesced so thoroughly that it was rarely ever mentioned. Even now Americans do not talk about it, so thoroughly was the regime of the unsayable inculcated during the second half of the past century. Rules defining the utterable and the unutterable continue to protect a system of beliefs, an ideology, from debilitating, disruptive questioning. They have been another symptom of fear. And they have brought a great poverty to American life.

To divide the public sphere between the acknowledged and the ignored, the explicit and the hidden, the declared and the furtive was not new to the Cold War era, nor is it an invention of public life unique to America. Rituals of confession and purgation—a fair description of the "un-American activities" hearings—are common in history. But they became a pronounced aspect of American life during the McCarthyist period. Along with much else, they introduced fear into the public sphere, so beginning a process of social privatization that would become more evident during the Cold War's later years. This is among the saddest aspects of Cold War man, for it shrank him intellectually to an extent we cannot fully appreciate because we continue to live with the consequences. One price of ideology is a regrettable narrowing of alternatives. A society leaves much unavailable to itself. This eventually produces internal weaknesses—another consequence of ideology. And we have not yet left behind the ideology that came into its fullness during the Cold War years.

———

It would be difficult to name a nation less desirous of "the aid of our character" than Vietnam after the French defeat in 1954. Americans no longer spoke in the Wilsonian idiom by the time the war in Southeast Asia escalated a decade later. They spoke of "winning hearts and minds," which amounted to the same thing. The mission was as it always had been: Others must be made to love us, and so desire emulation. In this case, Americans had to save the Vietnamese from their Vietnameseness: an unachievable aim that produced an unwinnable war.

Vietnam was the most prominent example of how the Cold War was fought in the 1960s and seventies. Europe was secure by way of a terrorizing balance of power between East and West, even if nuclear weapons had proved to be nothing more than a complication once both sides recognized that they were at bottom unusable. This left America with a kind of Hobson's choice. Obsessed with preserving its security and by this time its "credibility," it could engage in conventional warfare in exotic locales with all its science and machinery, but not to the point Moscow or Beijing would be provoked into a direct confrontation.

Vietnam, as all who recall the conflict there know, was a searing experience for Americans. Protracted, mortal in its casualty count, and less and less explainable as the years went by, it nearly rent America asunder. Afterward, some foreign policy scholars considered that it was not nearly as important as it had been thought to be at the time. On the other end of the argument, Henry Kissinger asserted that in Vietnam America found a test of its resolve that was more or less infinite. "Today, for the first time in history, we face the stark reality that the challenge is unending," Kissinger said late in the war. "We must learn to conduct foreign policy as other nations have had to conduct it for so many centuries—without escape and without respite. This condition will not go away."[26]

In some ways the thought was as American as July Fourth: the long challenge to remake the world in our image, such that we ourselves would never face the obligation to change. But Kissinger, who had always had a more European cast of mind than those around him, had also brought to the fore an essential contradiction in Wilsonianism in its "neo" iteration. Classical Wilsonian thinking had at its core the assumption that the policy would succeed itself out of existence. Once the world had been made safe for democracy, there would be no more need for crusades; the millenarian mission would be accomplished and a utopian future, global in character, would lie ahead. In this respect, Kissinger put his finger on a fundamental change in

American thinking: What was once an internationalism theoretically rooted in temporary crisis had become a permanent condition.

Any war that claims fifty-eight thousand lives on one side and several million on the other must be ranked as important. But the American defeat, as it has turned out, indeed did not matter much—not, at least, on maps, not in Southeast Asia. No row of dominoes fell. There was no worrisome standoff between Vietnam and the Southeast Asian nations that were effectively America's Cold War satellites in the region.

So we must look elsewhere for the meaning of the American defeat in Vietnam, for it was surely an event of magnitude. America's first defeat in modern war was less a military matter than a psychological and emotional shock: paradoxically, a domestic blow. It was a transparent war, America's first, and in its progress it deprived Americans of all claim to innocence. At its deepest level it thus brought our mythologically informed idea of ourselves into open contradiction with history. Conservatives used to argue that daily newscasts of war footage in American living rooms were costing America public support and morale, and they were right. The sight of American soldiers dying and the destruction of Vietnamese lives and land and villages proved to be too much, a kind of overload, for many Americans. Few had ever actually seen what the Cold War looked like. And when they did, science, the new altar at which Americans worshiped, proved to have a limit. These were two differences between the 1950s and the 1960s. In the prior decade the Cold War had little visuality—Korea, for instance: It was far less available to Americans, a faraway conflict. In the sixties, the American way and all its limitations were what you saw after work and before dinner—cocktail hour accompaniment.

The visual availability of the war was one factor—there were others—in bringing Americans near to a state of exhaustion in the matter of crusades. Exhaustion and a lapse in belief would be more precise. This created a psychological crisis among Americans that I do not think has yet been properly estimated. Americans lived by a legend of victory and success; they had never known frustration. The taste was especially bitter in that Americans had gone from isolation to dominance in a matter of decades and had never had to compete for the latter. Cynicism and irony seemed to smother any vigorous understanding of what was possible. What could be seen simply did not match the Wilsonian narrative of America the good and great, the mythical America. This was momentous, of historical importance. It meant, for one thing, that communism was losing its force as the everlasting enemy in America's imagery; it no longer gave Americans the fallout-shelter fear it did during the 1950s and early sixties. Yet more fundamentally in the period following the defeat in 1975, the pull of American mythology weakened—possibly for the first time since the nation's founding. Its leaders had proven pettily corrupt (Watergate), and they had conducted the war unwisely, recklessly, and dishonestly (the Pentagon Papers). American idealism grew distant, hollow, ever beyond the nation's grasp. If this is what it means to be the world's saving nation, many Americans may as well have said, we had better think again about the ideology that brought us to this point. And the year after Saigon "fell" and became Ho Chi Minh City, that is what Americans did when they elected Jimmy Carter to the presidency.

———

The Cold War still had many years left in it after 1975, of course. The Soviets and the Americans made a fetish of counting nuclear warheads, new weapons emerged, and strategic arms talks led to more strategic arms talks. While there were occasional proxy wars, such as in Angola and Nicaragua, the Cold War assumed a certain bureaucratic character. Other issues—Israel, Iran, oil, the emerging problem of imperial overstretch—began to require as much attention as Cold War tensions.

Carter was confident that the Cold War was in its final days when he took office. He envisioned a brighter, lighter, more cooperative world, much as Wendell Willkie, the prominent Republican attorney, anticipated when he published *One World* in 1943, and much as FDR had until his death two years later. "We have learned that we cannot and should not try to intervene militarily in the internal affairs of other countries unless our own nation is endangered," Carter asserted.[27] This had previously been among America's many unsayables. It was as much as to turn three decades of Cold War logic, beginning with the Truman Doctrine, on its head.

What Carter wanted instead was precisely what American policy makers and generals had ignored since 1898. He had the effrontery to suggest—another unsayable—that American behavior abroad should match its ideals. Unless American foreign policy reflected American values and principles, he said, "we make a mockery of those values." Justice, equity, and human rights could no longer be considered separately from matters of war and peace. One recalls the surprise many felt when Carter named an assistant secretary of state to look after human rights. There was a genuine novelty in the very thought of it, for human rights had not previously been accorded any place of consequence in Cold War diplomacy, statecraft, or foreign policy altogether. True, this can be painted as a variant strategy in prosecuting the Cold War, given Moscow's record in such matters. But Carter stood for something much larger. He understood and was willing to say that America had lost sight of its better idea of itself. His was a proposal to make the United States authentically what it had always claimed to be but had never been: a new kind of nation with ideals and democratic values that were the very objects of its policies.

Carter's one-term presidency, which suffered a dearth of dazzling moments, went down more or less in flames. Arms talks with the Soviets took on an acrimonious tone, while at home the defense establishment heckled Carter for being soft on communism and letting the Soviets overtake America in the nuclear weapons count. Carter got a strategic arms treaty signed early in 1979—only to ask Congress to defer passage after the Soviet invasion of Afghanistan at the end of the same year. There were other blots in Carter's copybook so far as Cold War Americans were concerned. He canceled the B-1 bomber project and the neutron bomb. In 1977 he signed a treaty agreeing to give control of the Panama Canal Zone back to Panama at century's end.

Carter's single world-class diplomatic accomplishment came in 1978, when Israel and Egypt signed peace accords at Camp David that endure to this day. But the sun did not shine long on the Carter presidency. In late 1979, not long after the shah was deposed, Iranian demonstrators seized the American embassy in Tehran and held seventy-six diplomats and staff captive for more than a year. Several months into the crisis, Carter approved a high-risk rescue attempt, the sort of thing a hardened post-Vietnam patriot might try. He sent a fleet of helicopters into the Iranian desert, but it never made Tehran: Sand fouled the engines and forced the aircraft down. Footage of them lying wrecked amid the Iranian dunes almost certainly provides one of the lasting images of the Carter administration, made the more poignant by the release of the hostages on Ronald Reagan's inauguration day the following year.

Carter's four-year stay in the White House, and all the attendant assumptions and imagery Americans now associate with it, is among the most unfortunate passages in the Cold War. He could have, with proper understanding from the public, the lobbies, the military, and the politicians, made so much more of his term. The defeat in Vietnam was the true psychological subtext of Carter's time in office. How should Americans understand it—this was the question. Carter could have turned April 1975 into an occasion for national reflection, reimagination, and renewal. He could have turned America away from its mythological conception of itself—which by this time was becoming insufferably destructive and self-defeating—and toward a historical idea of its place in the world. This, I believe, was Carter's intent, and also what Americans thought they wanted when they elected him. Few may understand Carter's vision in this fashion, but for it he will someday get his revisionist historian.

What happens when two nations enter into conflict and one emerges the victor and the other the vanquished? Many minds have turned to this question—mostly European minds—and the answer is not so simple as it may seem. But the question is highly relevant to the American case in Vietnam.

No nation enters into war or conflict without believing it will win. Equally, each nation that takes to the battlefield is fully invested in its worldview. Thus: We will win because of who we are and what we have accomplished in the world. This is the underlying assumption of all combatants. But victory and defeat are highly ambiguous states, as the writer Wolfgang Schivelbusch makes plain in *The Culture of Defeat*.[28] The vanquished are forced to reconsider their idea of themselves and their capabilities and limitations. Defeat has proven them wrong. So they must reimagine themselves as a people and also what place they hold in the world. They must enter into a thoroughgoing national analysis of their position. They must change. Defeat thus makes a people thoughtful. And it often leads to a new and more fertile challenge later on, either on or off the battlefield, for the vanquished always return—a new people with a renovated national ethos, an empathetic worldview that is a source of wisdom and strength.

As to the victors, they need change nothing, reconsider nothing, remake nothing. All that need be done is simply to continue on as before, harboring the illusions that victory means permanent victory and one need never alter anything. These are the natural assumptions of any triumphant nation. "History may in the short term be made by the victors, but historical wisdom is in the long run enriched more by the vanquished," a German historian wrote in the 1980s. "Being defeated appears to be an inexhaustible wellspring of intellectual progress."[29]

There are any number of historical instances to which this principle can be usefully applied. In an earlier essay I used a variant of the theme to compare Europe with the United States in the nineteenth century. The Europeans had failed in their revolutionary effort and embarked on a lengthy intellectual exploration of their predicament, while victorious Americans had no need of thinking so long as they could continue moving westward. The Spanish after 1898 are another case: Contemporary accounts convey the impression of a nation eased by the shedding of a long-borne burden and eager to move through history—the empire behind them—with a lighter step. One might note Japan after 1945 as a rather obvious addition to this list.

This goes precisely to the point of post-Vietnam America. It was a moment when the nation could have entered history and renewed itself, reversed itself—deconsecrated itself, one may say. This was Carter's invitation, properly understood. America came close, as it did in the 1890s. But it was not to be. There was too much at stake—something less than a cosmology but something more than a worldview, something near to a religion or an ideology, and Americans proved unable or unwilling to live without it. They chose instead an attempt to lunge rather desperately back in time. To do this they elected one of the most retrograde chief executives ever to occupy the White House: another "man of the West," nostalgic to the core, and unwilling to let go of simple verities more suited to the nineteenth century. Ronald Reagan not only stood for and deployed the old American myths: As it turned out he was himself a myth, a man of the imaginary present, perfect to play a leading role in the Cold War's final act.

———

"There are only two peoples now," Charles Augustin Sainte-Beuve wrote in 1847. "Russia is still barbarous, but it is great. The other young nation is America. The future is there between these two great worlds. Someday they will collide, and then we shall see struggles of which the past can give no idea."[30]

It is almost as if the French historian and critic saw forward a century and some years to read the mind of America's fortieth president. Ronald Reagan's fixation on the "evil empire" is well enough known, and it extends back far into his life before he entered the White House. He counted his determination to break the Soviet Union a crusade, with all the religious weight of this term well in mind. Reagan pushed defense spending up by a third, to $300 billion, in the first of his two terms (and by more than that in his second). In 1983 he announced the Strategic Defense Initiative, a missile defense system suspended in space (and hence known as Star Wars).

The odd thing to contemplate now is how little these expensive defense programs, as well as a great deal of Hollywood-derived rhetoric, changed the complexion of U. S.-Soviet relations. Washington and Moscow had more or less institutionalized the Cold War by Reagan's day. He attended summits and rounds of arms talks just as his predecessors had. It hardly bears mentioning, but Reagan cannot finally be awarded the credit he was to claim for staring down the Soviets and drawing the Cold War to a close. No outsider in any such circumstance can make such a claim. The fading of empires and great nations always reflects internal weaknesses and decay. In the worst of outcomes, Americans may learn this for themselves over the next couple of decades.

Reagan's true significance as president lay less in his defense budgets and his hostility to Moscow than in something less tangible but more lasting in its impact on American life and American thinking. More profoundly than anything else, Reagan was a psychological influence in a nation that had been knocked off its feet. Carter offered one response to the defeat in Vietnam—an honorable response, as I have already suggested. Reagan offered a more primitively satisfying alternative. He countered Carter's empathetic philosophy of courageous defeat with the delusional proposition that America could turn back. He offered Americans a posture that they could strike, a pose, an affect. Carter had invited Americans to enter into time, to assume a place in historical reality, to become a nation among other nations; his presidency was thus about genuine change. Reagan's message was that there was no need of change. The innocence America lost in Southeast Asia could be retrieved. America could return to the time that was out of time. It could retain all its myths and its exemption from history. Which of these men, then, represented an embrace of the future and which a retreat?

By the 1980s, defending American exceptionalism and the myths supporting it required skill in reading the fears and desires of Americans. A good management of imagery and symbols and an understanding of spectacle—altogether a cognizance of our culture of representation—had grown ever more important since Truman took on the Greek question in 1947. It was among our Cold War instruments of control as applied at home.[31] And it was the very stuff of politics once Reagan entered the White House. Through Reagan, Americans discovered how to make an abstraction of the Soviets and reconstruct them just as they had understood them to be in the 1940s. Patriotism had become, since Vietnam, a faint signal among many Americans. Reagan revived it—but as a matter more of affect than of conviction or belief. Without acknowledging defeat, he let Vietnam stand as one battle in the larger war for the world. Hence the sudden and drastic shift in the American psyche from the sympathetic earnestness represented by Carter to Reagan's rendition of might, masculinity, and determination. Politics at home as well as international politics became almost wholly symbolic, wholly gestural and spectacular: "Mr. Gorbachev, tear down this wall!" Reagan's years were a resort to representation as ambitious as any since the American century began. And among the problems of representation as I mean it in these essays is that it must be incessantly reiterated; otherwise its efficacy is lost.

Let us look again at nostalgia. It is interesting to count the varieties of it that Reagan evoked—some almost certainly by design, some perhaps unconsciously. There was a nostalgia for the frontier-era West that was bred into him during his Hollywood years. He used this to seductive effect during his public appearances. And many Americans were oddly taken with imagery that derived from film and fantasy, as if they could not distinguish between Hollywood's make-believe and the realties Americans were supposed to confront in Washington. There was another kind of nostalgia for the early Cold War period, when American supremacy was unquestioned, when science met all challenges, and when one was either with America or against it. There was (yet again) a nostalgia for the peaceful, pastoral, disengaged America of the nineteenth century and of the post–World War I period. And there was a kind of disinterred nostalgia for World War II. This last would blossom once more after the Cold War's end, when Americans were desperate to remember themselves in the twentieth century but when it had become difficult to face the multiple tones of gray that tinted the nation's Cold War performance.

The Reagan administration furnished a war to enhance this new givenness to looking back with blurred vision. In the autumn of 1983 and with considerable fanfare, U.S. troops invaded the Caribbean island of Grenada after a social democratic government of no particular harm or import took power. The intent was to demonstrate America's post–Vietnam prerogative while also putting a victory on American television screens. The problem with Grenada was that one could hardly call it a war. It was something closer to an act of thoughtless discourtesy, setting aside the bombing of a foster home in which scores of children died. But one draws from that brief escapade a sense of what Reagan and those around him thought the country needed to see: an extension of American power where Americans chose to extend it, a risk-free victory not unlike Cuba in 1898. In Grenada, as in Cuba, it was war as spectacle—"a hippodrome affair," as Teddy Roosevelt had put it.

In the post–Vietnam, post-Carter, post-Reagan era, the last's proclivity for representation and semiotic reference has persisted to a startling extent. It is large in his legacy. Imagery and spectacle have all but taken over from any thoughtful appraisal of America's circumstances. This has been the consequence of a national acceptance of a self-consciously constructed image of America that Reagan encouraged more than any modern president before or after his two terms. It consisted of two elements characteristic of the Cold War, and I have already dwelt upon them: Science in an odd combination with nostalgia, the looking forward and the looking back. And in Reagan, at the Cold War's far end, they crystallized. One can measure this by way of Star Wars, a hocus-pocus project from the start, and in the beginnings of a national obsession with "terrorism" as the Cold War started to wind down in the mid-1980s. The question then is the question now: Can America survive without an enemy? The judgment so far appears to be no, it must somehow have one if America as an idea is to cohere.

There are two other aspects of Reagan's legacy that are worthy of consideration. I was living abroad during Reagan's White House years—a fact I mention simply because it gave me the advantage of detachment, of unfamiliarity within familiarity, on my journeys home. On those occasions I could not help but notice the progressive privatization of the American personality. Almost surely this was a reflection of one of Reagan's various nostalgias, for it appeared to be occurring in the name of "traditional" frontier individualism as such myths had taken shape over a long period of time. But its impact was vastly more than sentimental. It was a measure of an alarming atomization in American society. It signaled a purposeful corrosion of the public sphere. "Greed is good," one suddenly heard—first in a film, then in our national conversation. It was a thought so foreign and obtuse that it will ever after be associated with the strange climate Reagan and those around him had cultivated. The period consolidated an American faith in the infallibility of markets, and it portrayed government as belonging to someone other than Americans, ever part of the problem, never part of the solution. But for all its forceful assertions, the period was one of denial. Margaret Thatcher, Britain's prime minister during Reagan's time in office, put the creed best for both of them. "And who is society? There is no such thing!" she famously asserted. "There are individual men and women and there are families."[32]

We still live, in some measure, according to the precepts that arose, consciously or unconsciously, during the Reagan years. They gave us the financial collapse of 2008, it is fair to say, and left us ill-equipped to advance decisively beyond it. They are plainly inflected in our national political debate. Reagan opened the door to a radically unsustainable idea of the individual, one based almost entirely on myths that had begun to fade. And it is equally hard to miss the other tendency Reagan brought to the fore in American politics. He wanted not only to restore the American spirit; he also wanted to inspire a revival of religious spirit—specifically the Christian spirit—among Americans. "What I have felt for a long time is that people in this country were hungry for what you might call a spiritual revival," Reagan once told a reporter. "And I decided that if it was possible for me to help in that revival, I wanted to do that."[33]

Religion has never been far from the surface in American public life, of course. As noted in an earlier essay, it was, with republicanism, one of the prominent strands in early American thought. Winthrop, Edwards, Wilson, Reagan, the younger Bush: They were all on the same American errand. But it was the American century that brought religion explicitly into the political sphere. To Wilson in 1912, God had selected America "to show the way to the nations of the world how they should walk in the paths of liberty."[34] Here is Eisenhower four decades later: "Recognition of the Supreme Being is the first, most basic expression of Americanism. Without God there would be no American form of government, nor an American way of life."[35] A year after this remark and amid much controversy, Eisenhower signed a law making "In God We Trust" America's official motto.

The religious rhetoric was common enough throughout the American century—an important component of its psychological foundations, as Wilson indicated it would be. And there can be few better illustrations of the way history can be invented than the blurring of church and state in the name of patriotism, notably since the Cold War's onset. In another idiom, both Eisenhower and Reagan could have been speaking in the seventeenth century. But not in the eighteenth: None of America's founding documents—Paine's *Common Sense,* the Declaration of Independence, the *Federalist Papers,* the Constitution, and so on—left any room for a deity as a source of political inspiration or authority. The divine right of monarchs, indeed, was among the things the new nation most wanted to leave behind. There was plenty of religion in the air when those first texts were written, but it wafted through American life, as Tocqueville noted, quite independent of the state and politics. Reagan's hyper-American stance might be taken as profoundly un-American—as has been so much of what has since arisen from it—except that the odd-colored thread itself has long been woven into the American tradition.[36]

The vital question becomes why this long confusion, as old as the republic, reemerged with such prevalence toward the end of the twentieth century. In my view it was a response to new uncertainties. Members of the Reagan administration spoke often of themselves as the manifestation of a renewed self-confidence in America. The "Vietnam syndrome," as America's disillusionment after the war was called, had been conquered. It was "morning in America." The nation could push out its chest again. I do not accept this interpretation of the time. As I read it, Reagan's administration betokened just the opposite of its claim. The recourse to religion, the rise of fundamentalism, the appearance of Bible-toting politicians, the cowboy imagery the administration cultivated, the penny-ante war that reeked of a reenactment of Cuba in 1898—it all suggested that as a nation Americans were insecure as to their providential inheritance and their exemption from history's temporalities. As the century drew to a close, then, an apparent confidence reflected deep apprehension. And for good reason: History was near, but Americans still wanted to believe they were exempt from it.

———

Sainte-Beuve was right when he identified Russia and America as two poles in a world-engulfing struggle for supremacy. He understood the enormity of the rivalry to come. But the two empires collided only indirectly, by way of third world proxy wars, or through the immense apparatus of espionage and intelligence each side maintained. As to Reagan, after he left office—already suffering from Alzheimer's disease, according to his son—the man and his time appeared to evaporate. Republicans of a certain stripe quickly made him a mythical figure, and the imagery seemed to be enough. But an odd evanescence—perhaps the result of so much actorly posturing—seemed to enfold his years in office. Little of what he said has proven memorable or of lasting use. "There you go again" has endured, but of course this was pure gesture. It is as if Reagan were made for his moment and no other. It is as if Americans never truly knew who Reagan was—an impression underscored when his official biographer, unable to discover the authentic man behind the imagery, produced a work of fiction.

Many things can be listed among the Cold War's consequences. It left America more depleted—materially and psychologically—than it understood itself to be. As others have written, it was a half-century of lost opportunity when one considers the incalculable cost of it. It left the nation in physical disrepair and badly distorted by way of its scientific research programs. It left Americans with a defense budget that is of near sacred status despite our condition of imperial overstretch. The Cold War line between the sayable and unsayable continues to circumscribe our public discourse. Forty percent of America's industrial production is now related directly or indirectly to defense spending. And reckless is the elected official who says it should be otherwise.[37]

Where does this leave Americans now? What does the recent past make of us? The Cold War left behind something of that child-like quality that I have mentioned—a result of the era's new ideas as to power, authority, and participation in public life. The larger question is this: Are we, the descendants of Cold War man, capable of the tasks before us in a new century? Can Americans put aside the mythical self and assume a historical self? The second half of the past century left Americans so impoverished and depleted, so wanting in imagination, so easily satisfied with facility at a moment when the facile is not enough, that the Cold War is best understood as a long and fateful delay in America's historical development.

Much of this is still evident in American life. But there is one dimension of the Cold War and its legacy that remains especially deserving of attention. This has to do with its most basic nature. Was it a modern war, as we unfailingly think of it, or was it at the core primitive? The Cold War marks out a forty-four-year period. Did America advance or regress in the course of those years? Was it different at the end than at the beginning?

Writers such as John Dewey, perhaps reflecting their Americanism, tend to offer a simple idea of the modern human being. To be a modern man is commonly taken to mean having developed materially and technologically. It means "the machinery of his new arts of production and transportation," to use a phrase from *The Quest for Certainty*. It meant, as Dewey used the term in 1929, "action." It meant humankind's ability to exert itself upon the world so as to make a secure place within it.[38]

Primitive man was incapable of such action. There was no question of exerting oneself upon the world so as to alter it. Primitive man existed defenseless amid all the earth's dangers and uncertainties. "For primitive men had none of the elaborate arts of protection and use which we now enjoy and no confidence in his own powers when they were reinforced by appliances of art," Dewey wrote. "He lived under conditions in which he was extraordinarily exposed to peril, and at the same time he was without the means of defense which are to-day a matter of course."[39]

Dewey, like nearly everyone alive at the time, was profoundly affected by the rapid arrival of the modern in all its manifestations—aesthetic, scientific, technological, sociological, philosophic, industrial. His definition of what it means to be modern, then, cannot surprise us. Many of us today may, indeed, adhere to it. It is, in addition, the perfect Cold War definition of modernity, given its implicit idolatry of science and the material and mechanical arts. But it is at best an incomplete definition and is very possibly wrong altogether.

What, then, makes a people authentically modern? I have touched upon this in a previous essay. It has to do with a people's relationship with time—and by extension with politics, which occurs in time. A modern society is one that has given up its resistance to history—cruel, relentless history. It is, by contrast, accepting of the reality that people alone make history. There is no looking upward for salvation in such a society. There is no looking backward in search of a redemptive time past to which one can hope to return. There are no such myths. Instead, there is an assumption of responsibility by way of politics. Neither time nor history is to be transcended. Indeed, there is an acceptance of life's infinite relativity and its many limitations. The meaning of any given historical event is rooted in that event alone.

What kind of societies entered upon the Cold War, it is now time to ask. Both were millennial in their fundamental character. The Soviets, at least in theory, promised an ultimate salvation by means of a return to an archaic golden age—a sort of Eden, organized as communism in its perfected form. But it is the Americans who concern us. And when one considers all they said and did in waging the Cold War, it must be counted, again, the promise of a return to a perfected, untroubled world—another kind of utopia. "Make it like that of New England," Winthrop's phrase, was still the project.

The Depression of the nineteen thirties brought America as close as it had ever come to a fully historicist view of itself. Circumstances forced this. It amounted to the most searching self-examination Americans had ever attempted—more thorough, even, than that attempted during the Progressive era. World War II sent the nation on another providential mission, and the war's end was therefore a rather key moment. What would America be after 1945? It is the question Wendell Willkie anticipated by a few years and Carter would pose in another context three decades later. At its core the question was one of history: Would America know itself as "part of the whole," as Willkie put it, a nation among other nations, or would it revert to its national mythology and set out for the next crusade?

We have our answer, of course. The crusade lasted half a century and cost millions of lives and trillions of dollars. In its essence it was a reply to history. One of its purposes—not to be subordinated—was to counter the advances of the New Deal years. This left America in a pre-historicist condition at an unusually late moment in the modern era. America was a modern nation with features of a premodern society prominent within it. This produced an identifiably American personality. Americans were unable to understand events but by interpretation, blind to history's course, deaf to the voices of others.

———

We are all more or less familiar with the myth of Narcissus. Born of a nymph, "he had a beauty that broke hearts," to quote from Ted Hughes's version of Ovid. There was a question whether the boy could survive with such perfect features. "Yes," replied Tiresias, the blind seer, "unless he learns to know himself."[40]

And therein lay the fate of Narcissus. One day he glanced at his reflection in a perfectly still pool of water. He was captivated by his own image:

> Not recognizing himself
> He wanted only himself. He had chosen

From all the faces he had ever seen
Only his own. He was himself
The torturer who now began his torture.

Narcissus is inaccessible to himself: When he reaches down to touch his image, he disturbs the water and his reflection disappears. He eventually dies, just as Tiresias had foreseen. But there is a part of the Narcissus myth that is often overlooked. Early in his manhood he had met a nymph named Echo, who was capable only of repeating back to Narcissus his own words. This drove Narcissus slightly mad:

"No," he cried, "no, I would sooner be dead
Than let you touch me."

There is something in this ancient Greek tale that is revealing of America at the Cold War's end. It had spent fifty years staring at its own reflection, unable to see anything or anybody else. Equally, given its treatment of so many aspiring democracies, it is fair to say it could not bear to hear back from others the ideals it had professed itself, from the Philippines onward. America, as Wilson had warned, had wanted others to accept from it only an image of itself.

This was America at the Cold War's end: unable to touch even its own image, unable to make out the images of others, unable to hear what others were saying. In history, two early signs that a great power is in danger of decline are when it goes blind and when it goes deaf. America by the early 1990s still did not think historically. So it was blind even to its blindness, deaf to its deafness. This was how Cold War man turned out.

———

The 1990s were an aberrant decade for many Americans. The Cold War was over, although it is highly debatable to suggest that America was the victor. Suddenly there was no enemy, and America seemed to flounder. The Cold War had not left behind the utopian environment that triumph was supposed to bring. Instead, Americans woke up to a world far more complex than the Cold War decades had been, and the Cold War had left them unprepared for complexity. In Russia a pronounced nostalgia for Stalin rose to the surface. Americans found this very odd, but a corresponding nostalgia for the Cold War and its simple presumptions was nearly as evident among them.

There was much triumphalism in the air as the 1990s progressed. Francis Fukuyama, a State Department functionary at the time, announced grandly that the world had reached "the end of history."[41] This was considered a novel observation, though it was simply a restatement of the "end of ideology" argument in fashion in the 1950s and 1960s. Fukuyama meant that it was no longer feasible to imagine a world nearer to perfection than one founded on the liberal principles America had long held so dear. The task, as it always had been, was to preserve things just as they were and bear the message around the globe. Fukuyama had many critics (and deserved every one), but the thesis captivated Washington, Wall Street, and many prominent publicists. It returned America to its exceptional role; it restored America's capacity to take up the old myths once again.

America found another mission at this time in the phenomenon known as globalization. Globalization in its 1990s iteration meant Americanization: It was a one-way street. It meant private enterprise, reduced state sectors, minimal regulation, and ungoverned markets free to operate according to their own semisacred forces. These became totemic values for many Americans—objects of primitive belief. America's time as "the sole superpower" was brief: Americans seem to have been the only ones who expected it to last very long. But for its short reign it reigned in the name of free markets rather than democracy, for in the end, Americans told the world, they came to the same thing. In time, many nations took to calling this regime "market fundamentalism" or (an Argentinian coinage) "savage capitalism."

In a certain way, globalization was merely a continuation of the Cold War by other means. Americans could not accept in others any way but their own way. The best example is social democracy, with its advocacy of a mixed economy and its emphasis on the common maintenance of public goods. It was one of America's true enemies in both the Cold War and the decade that followed. Americans, indeed, have never been able to bear this quintessentially nineteenth-century political form. Social democracy is, among much else, historicist. This is one reason it has always repelled so many Americans. The very term can be counted among our enduring unsayables. Certainly, social democracy in any of its varied forms was the principal adversary during the 1990s: All neoliberal precepts were aimed at its destruction. During the Cold War, at least as many social democracies fell to American might or covert sabotage as did socialist or communist nations. Washington could not tolerate it, it has always seemed to me, because it represented a credible, historically rooted alternative to the American variety of liberalism—the "fragment," to call upon Louis Hartz's term again, that America took from eighteenth-century Europe.

———

Among the many curious aspects of the decade after the Cold War was the way Americans took to remembering and forgetting. The Cold War had turned Americans into the world's greatest forgetters. America's collective way of managing the memory of the atomic bombings in Japan set the pattern for half a century. "America felt both deep satisfaction and deep anxiety, and these responses have co-existed ever since," Robert J. Lifton and Greg Mitchell wrote in *Hiroshima in America*. "Half a century later, Americans continue to experience pride, pain, and confusion over the use of the atomic bomb against Japan."[42] Indeed, an effort to commemorate Hiroshima in 1995 became so politically fraught that the Smithsonian Institution had to drop all plans to mark the occasion.

Hiroshima and its aftermath were a kind of template. There was the remembering and forgetting of the occasion, side by side. There were, as Lifton and Mitchell noted, pride, pain, confusion, and denial. I would add hubris, guilt, and shame. All these emotions and others were what Americans lived with simultaneously throughout the Cold War. Mossadegh in Iran, Arbenz in Guatemala, Lumumba in the Congo, Allende in Chile: Many of us do not even know the names, but they were all legitimate leaders felled by transgressive American designs. In time, there was a numbing effect and a regret—a kind of secret, unsayable regret—as to how America had come to use its power. This lay just beneath the oddly placid surface of the Cold War as Americans lived it from day to day. Some Americans, surely, took note that American power had made the world less secure than it had been, less safe, and altogether less livable and humane. But this is not part of the way we remember ourselves.

It is near to inevitable that such a passage in human history would lead to certain pathologies. Here I would like to explore one having to do with the awakening of memory among Americans after a long Cold War slumber. I choose this element of the Cold War—effect and aftereffect—because the way Americans resolve the question of remembering the twentieth century will have much to do with their fate in the twenty-first.

In the mid-1990s, an odd and oddly self-indulgent phenomenon arose in America—and, so far as I know, only in America. It is still with us. This was the appearance of the personal memoir in such plentitude that it was swiftly declared a new literary genre— "reality-based literature," as the *New York Times* called it. Great claims were made for the memoir. It represented the democratization of the written word, because everyone has a story and, as with a harmonica, anyone can make a sound. In *When Memory Speaks,* the memoirist Jill Ker Conway claimed that we could no longer surrender our disbelief to works of fiction and that subjects such as psychology, philosophy, culture, and so on were lost to us because scholarly discourse was of necessity inaccessible. "Autobiography," Conway wrote, "is almost the only kind of writing which tackles such questions in language a non-specialist can read."[43]

This last is an audaciously indefensible statement, and it misses entirely the problem raised by contemporary American memoirs. This problem is easily stated: Memoir in its new American form represents a retreat from public to personal remembering. There is the desire to remember, but not to remember commonly shared events, for the public events that lie behind us are often too fraught to recall or discuss. One might easily become—dreaded condition—political in one's remembering. The memoir of the kind I am considering is almost exclusively concerned with family, childhood, personal grief, or personal triumph. Rare, indeed, is the memoir that wades into the ocean of the forgotten facts of public life during the Cold War years.

It comes, in short, to the privatization of history. This is what numerous of our memoirs, dozens per season, induce. It is their secret purpose. And to understand this we need go back only to 1967, when André Malraux published his *Anti-Memoirs.* Malraux disliked the memoir as personal confession (hence his title). An intensely public man, he had no interest in "the pursuit of secrets," as he put it. "What do I care about what matters only to me?" Malraux asked. "What interests me in any man is the human condition. And in all of them certain characteristics which express not so much an individual personality as a particular relationship with reality."[44]

To live in a state of unofficially enforced forgetting constitutes a trauma, as any citizen of the former Eastern bloc can tell you. In the American case, coming awake has meant looking back at last on a half-century shrouded in the mists of secrecy and misinformation. There was, on the one hand, an idealized self-portrait at stake. In addition, there was the prospect of discovering that we were not who we thought we were or had been. So often, we would have found, America's successes came to its failures; our victories so often turned out to be our defeats. The American-managed coup in Iran in 1953 eventually produced an Islamic state; our coup in Guatemala a year later led to a bloody insurgency of several decades' duration. But as it spread the economic gospel of neoliberalism in the 1990s, America chose to remember little of the previous fifty years. It still had no need to, having persuaded itself of its victory.

Memory, indeed, is a dangerous place to visit. Looking back requires that a people are willing to go forward by a different path, depending on what they see.

———

Not quite a century ago, Van Wyck Brooks, then a young Progressive-era literary critic, wrote an influential essay entitled "On Creating a Usable Past."[45] It has not since lost its importance in the American conversation. But what did Brooks mean? How does one create a past? What is a usable one? And to what purpose, this usable past?

Brooks was of a literary bent, but as a Progressive he shared with many of his generation a desire to build a new kind of future in America. Brooks published his essay in 1918, exactly two decades after America made its fateful choice between empire abroad and democracy at home. He shared with others of his generation a hope that America could still make itself a modern democracy by accommodating the realities of contemporary life, leaving mythological missions behind, and proceeding in a new direction.

But a new direction forward required a new past. This was Brooks's breakthrough insight. It meant looking back at the past not as a fixed tradition, firmly established and chiseled in stately stone. It meant entering the past creatively, with imagination, such that what one remembers may have been buried by those of a different time and sensibility. What was once determining of a society's character might fall into the background, and what was once considered of little account might come decisively to the fore. "What ought we elect to remember?" Brooks asked. It goes straight to the point. The past as anyone in any society remembers it is only a version of that past. Remembering is a kinetic activity—this was what Brooks understood. And how a society remembers itself will determine the direction it will take in the future. "For the spiritual past has no objective reality," Brooks wrote. "It yields only what we are able to look for in it."

Brooks describes our moment with a canny accuracy, because his remarks bear in them a truth that has meaning for all generations everywhere. But they are of special significance now to us—we Americans who stand with the Cold War behind us and a new and different century ahead.

How, then, to proceed?

Our past as we have it now is of little use to us. It is too much at odds with events as others understand them—as they were, indeed. There is vastly too much missing from it. We share a specific past with Indonesians, Guatemalans, and Iranians, for instance. But their pasts and ours are not the same in any of these cases or in dozens of others. This comes to hold us back. It isolates us. Too much in our own history of the American century, notably its second half, has been obliterated or fabricated—which comes to the same thing. And this kind of manufactured history comes to cause the opposite of the intended effect. At the time of invention, it causes events to disappear—or to appear in a favorable light. But this is a temporary result. Over time, it causes occluded events to linger in the memories of others—and, indeed, in the unconscious of at least some of us. Others have no recognized record of things as they actually happened, for we have deprived them of this. History has become a product for Western export, as a noted French thinker put it not long ago.[46] In consequence, others must retain events in their minds until history is properly recorded. This is how Americans stand among others today. Just as Americans live in the state of history without memory, many others thus live in a state of memory without history.

To repeat the question with this in mind, then, what is the way forward for Americans?

Let us consider the three kinds of history Bernard Lewis, the noted historian of the Middle East, once distinguished in some of his lectures.[47] One is remembered history, meaning recollections of a living tradition, the classics of a given culture, scripture, and so on. The second type Lewis calls recovered history. This means history once forgotten (for one reason or another) but later rediscovered and reconstructed. The third of Lewis's types is invented history. "This is history for a purpose," Lewis wrote, "a new purpose different from previous purposes." It might be made up, Lewis adds, or it may be found—"come upon." All three of these types are to be identified everywhere throughout the history of the human community.

Are Lewis's categories of use to us? Inventing history is a constant temptation, and some of our media and some of our popular historians and biographers indulge it. But even with a constructive intent it is too dangerous an endeavor, it seems to me, and the past we are considering is too proximate. But what about "recovering" a past that is usable in the way Brooks intended the term: a past that opens us to the community of nations in new, imaginative ways, such that we might be able to take a different place in the world and unburden ourselves of much in history that now weighs heavily upon us? Would it be possible for Americans to recover a history of the twentieth century that would be shorn of myths, stories, erasures, and fabrications?

It is difficult to pose these questions. Many are those who think the past as we now have it, even the Cold War past, is in no need of change or reexamination. Many, too, are those who understand the need for revision and pursue it honorably. But Americans have yet to be pushed or guided decisively beyond their idea of themselves as exceptional in human history, and it remains a question whether this would be possible—whether Americans would accept it. A novelist friend with an acute gift for historical understanding put it to me in blunt terms one day as I prepared to begin these essays. "What you propose," he said, "would be unbearable."

I do not think this is so. The things required are two, and the question is whether we have these things among us and in us.

First, consider again those two virtues C. Vann Woodward identified as desirable in the contemporary American historian. He named sympathy and detachment. What did he mean by this? The dead are in no need of sympathy, and our detachment from those who have come before us, however great our admiration, is complete. Woodward meant, plainly enough, sympathy for and detachment from us, us the living, in whose name our history is written. He meant that we had to learn how to convey historical experience without letting our beliefs, our stories, and our myths deface it beyond recognition and usefulness. Consider again our nineteenth-century historians—and many others in more recent times—in this light. The failures have been many. "They must have established some measure of immunity from the fevers and prejudices of their own times," Woodward wrote in describing the historians he had in mind, "particularly those bred of nationalism, with all its myths and pretensions, and those born of hysteria that closes the mind to new ideas of all kinds."[48]

The task of the historian in our time, in other words, is dis-illusionment—that is, to free Americans of their illusions about themselves. Some of these were identified quite early in the Cold War era. Denis Brogan, a British scholar in American studies, wrote a noted essay for *Harper's* in 1952 entitled "The Illusion of American Omnipotence."[49] Infinite power was our greatest illusion, Brogan considered. That same year Reinhold Niebuhr published *The Irony of American History*. To him, innocence and virtue were America's predominating illusions. "We have dreamed of a purely rational ad-justment of interests in human society; and we are involved in 'total' wars," Niebuhr wrote. "We have dreamed of a 'scientific' approach to all human problems; and we find that the tensions of a worldwide conflict release individual and collective emotions not easily brought under control. We had hoped to make neat and sharp distinctions between justice and injustice; and we discover that even the best hu-man actions involve some guilt."[50]

Omnipotence, innocence, virtue: We still live with a measure of illusion as to all three. It is the historian's task to cast such matters in a new light. "America has had cynical disparagement of her ideals from foreign, unfriendly, or hostile critics," Woodward concluded. "But she desperately needs criticism from historians of her own who can penetrate the legend without destroying the ideal, who can dis-pel the illusion of pretended virtue without dumping the genuine virtue."[51]

Woodward wrote in 1953, Brogan and Niebuhr a year earlier. And as these dates suggest, the early 1950s was a fertile period for such reflections—for writers willing to write against their time. The Cold War was new, and as the literature of the period indicates, there were many who found much in it to question. And now, standing beyond the Cold War's far end, we find these thoughts useful once again. What we need—the second imperative if we are to reconstruct or recover our past—is the will to change course and find a new and more workable future than the one that appears to lie before us now.

This is the choice—or one of them, at any rate—that faces Americans as I write these pieces. It is admittedly difficult to imagine a changed past and therefore a different future in our current political, social, and economic climate. But as much can be said of all great nations when they reach a certain hour in their afternoons. Change comes hard. Some do not transcend their own orthodoxies—their myths and stories, their expectations and assumptions, their histories as these are conventionally understood. It is then that decline comes. It is then they go deaf and blind, for nations of this kind are living according to apparent truths that no longer apply, and the world, in a great rush to find the future, passes them by.

But such a fate is in no wise an imperative. Other nations, just past the pinnacle of their powers and influence, find it within themselves to reassess their circumstances—where they have been and where they are. And for them, advancing into a new passage of their history, vitally and imaginatively, becomes not merely possible, but transforming.

TIME AND TIME AGAIN

——

An era can be said to end when its basic illusions are exhausted.
—Arthur Miller, "The Year It Came Apart," 1974

On the morning of September 11, 2001, I was in my study starting to write a syndicated column—a twice-a-week chore at that time. It was a balmy, comfortable Tuesday. We lived, then, on a small farm in rural Connecticut. If memory serves, I was planning to produce a commentary on Japanese politics.

"Come quickly," my wife called from the kitchen. "Something's happened." An urgency in her voice stirred me instantly.

The kitchen was where the radio was, generally tuned to the national news station. We listened. The reporting was not altogether coherent—it could not be at that early, outsized moment—but it seemed a plane had collided with one tower of the World Trade

Center in New York's financial district. Probably a private craft that lost its course, I recall saying.

"I think it's more than that," my wife replied.

In a few moments this became clear. In a few moments more the second tower in New York was hit. And in a few more a plane crashed into the Pentagon. A fourth plane went down in Pennsylvania. Soon enough, it was clear that America had been attacked by self-styled suicide combatants.

One did not know immediately what to think, given how far these events lay from one's most extravagant imaginings. Or perhaps it was a case of too many thoughts at once. There was a contradiction. The enormity of what had happened 112 miles from our house seemed too much to manage. At the same time, the fear and apprehension one felt that morning were faintly familiar: We had been trained to live within these emotions. What had happened was a strange, undreamed of variant of what we had always been told would happen. An enemy had come. It was unconsciously expected, so reifying an old national narrative, the narrative of American separateness. But it was wholly unexpected at the same time: Such an event could not have been otherwise. Part of what one ever after recalls at such moments is their confusion. Perplexity was an intimate feature of that morning, and so it is in part the subject of this essay.

We decided to walk. We climbed a hill along a country road to a place where we often stopped to look back at the farm. At that moment, its placidity, its wholeness, its fixedness in its place, suddenly seemed preposterous—complacent in a way that was somehow reprehensible. On the way back, we spoke of America and Americans and Americans' place in the world. These sorts of subjects had long been on our minds. Now, it seemed, another chapter had opened, but what would be said in it? What of the chapter that may just then have closed?

Behind the farmhouse was a meadow, and beyond that a dense forest. A little while after we returned, the kitchen radio still giving forth a flood of news, something I had never seen and never thought of seeing appeared. An army helicopter with camouflage paint flew low across our meadow and began making concentric loops above the forest. This went on for the better part of an hour. I understood by then: There was a regional airport roughly forty miles distant; this was military reconnaissance.

I have certain associations with helicopters. A cousin flew them in Indochina during the 1960s—sometimes in uniform, sometimes (over Laos or Cambodia) in blue jeans and a T-shirt with no markings or military tags. When I was small, my father used to park at the edge of the regional airfield—it was an army base then—and watch the aircraft come and go. They were large and faintly exotic to a small boy, of another world. Later in life, I saw the same footage as everyone else of Vietnam and numerous other war zones—always far distant, so often featuring helicopters. So much of what America did in those years was far away. We had so little consciousness of it. The technology was interesting, and that is what mesmerized us. But how innocent so many Americans had become. With what combination of innocence and irresponsibility had so many of us come to be colonized?

The sight of that helicopter, banking in graceful circles above a forest I knew by way of long walks or hunting deer in the autumns, gave me an insight I may not have come to for many months. And it has never left me. It was the complete incongruity of the scene. My surrounding woods had become, theoretically and for a little while, a potential zone of conflict. I thought of that noted line from Toynbee: History is something unpleasant that happens to other people, he once wrote. We are comfortably outside of all that.

And so did we think in our time. But the horrific collisions we had heard about on the radio that morning marked another collision of greater magnitude, if we can count it as such. With a weird, never-to-be-expected precision—8:46 A.M., Tuesday, September 11, 2001—the American century came to an end. This was so not because of the radical savagery of the attacks, or the long, horrific aftermath. It was so because at that moment America joined the world at last. This is to say it surrendered on September 11 all claims to immunity or exception. Its dream of eternal triumph had been ruptured. America's long mythological notion of itself had crumbled along with the Manhattan towers. The footage of the towers fascinated us, indeed, partly because their collapse was a kind of objective correlative for what had just happened to us. From those moments onward, America became part of history.

I did not mourn the passing of our myths, though I knew that this crumbling of a national self-image would contribute to the anguish many Americans would feel, even if this dimension of their sadness was altogether unconscious. I considered this inevitable—a kind of sorrow familiar to many throughout history but never before felt by Americans. The moment, or one like it, could not have been avoided perpetually.

Neither did I mourn the three thousand who died that day—not directly, not them alone. It seemed an incomplete gesture—partial in both meanings of the term—and I could not. I mourned instead all those who had died as a consequence of the American century. And those in the World Trade Center's towers and at the Pentagon and on a flight downed over Pennsylvania were a very small number of them. This, it seemed to me, was to think historically. It was a completed gesture—humane but whole and cognizant. It seemed the best way to mark America's exit from its century and its entrance into time, for America had run out of time and straight into time all at once.

———

"We are all Americans," *Le Monde* famously declared in its page-one headline on the morning of September 13. The gesture was considerate. But the French, I recall thinking at the time, had it exactly right and exactly upside down.

Jean-Marie Colombani, the Paris daily's editor, compared the moment to Kennedy's noted *"Ich bin ein Berliner"* declaration in 1962. But the two occasions were not at all the same and supported no such comparison. No one had joined America on September 11. No one had crossed the great divide distinguishing America from adversaries and allies alike. No one had entered into its mythologies, or its version of history; no one had offered dispensation for the prerogative America had long assumed. It was quite the opposite on September 11. It was America that crossed the divide it had erected, America that saw its version of history brutally contradicted, America that was to find its claim to be the world's "sole superpower" turn to ashes. This is what I mean when I say it was America that joined the world on September 11 and not the other way around.

Colombani made a subtle reference to this point in his editorial. He seemed to suggest that the September 11 attacks were to be understood as Cold War collateral damage—as, indeed, they were. "But the reality is perhaps also that of an America whose own cynicism has caught up with it," Colombani wrote. "If bin Laden, as the American authorities seem to think, really is the one who ordered the September 11 attacks, how can we fail to recall that he was in fact trained by the CIA and that he was an element of a policy, directed against the Soviets, that the Americans considered to be wise? Might it not then have been America itself that created this demon?"[1]

So much for "Nous sommes tous Américains." Intentionally or otherwise, *Le Monde* underscored an aspect of September 11 that bore within it a kind of subliminal bitterness. It had all happened by way of America's creations turned against it. It was all the outcome of the world America had fashioned in the second half of the twentieth century. Bin Laden was a creature of America's crusade against Soviet communism—the holiest of America's wars to date. Yet bin Laden had struck back at his creator—not in some remote desert outpost but at the very heart of the nation's most symbolic institutions, the houses wherein it honored its fortunes and its power. To make the point still clearer, bin Laden's chosen means were the sciences and technologies America had celebrated since the *Maine* had anchored in Havana harbor and TR had worn his saber into the jungle. The American century had begun by way of a nation's impulse to parade its practical superiority before the world, proclaiming the primacy of material accomplishment among human values. We will never know what perverse irony may have possessed Osama bin Laden as he planned his attacks on America with the products of its own industry.

Anyone alive and paying attention when the September 11 attacks occurred will recall the extraordinary mix of emotions Americans displayed. There were sorrow and grief, of course. There was fear. There were also anger and frustration. These are quite predictable responses to so horrific a tragedy—the horror and the tragedy both made endlessly available on national television afterward. Other feelings and reactions: There was disbelief. How could this have come to be in such intimate American geographies? There was confusion. Somehow to be American at that moment meant something different than it had meant twenty-four hours earlier. All the triumph Americans had felt since the Berlin Wall fell in 1989 had come to nothing. Americans were suddenly reminded—irrefutably, in a way that could not be glossed—that there was hatred abroad, that not everyone approved of "the indispensable nation," not everyone wanted to follow, not everyone admired our "character" or wanted the aid of it.

Amid all these reactions and recognitions, those concerning history and myth were not well understood. There comes a moment when national or societal myths exhaust themselves, or—better put—history overcomes them. When one believes in a myth it is not as a myth. It is believed in as a truth—a revealed truth. Then history advances, and myth must be understood to be as it is: a narrative that is in essence imaginary, symbolic, and from the beginning destined to be exposed. This is history's ineluctable consequence. But myths are historical phenomena, as earlier noted; they occur in time and exert a force. A people may still keep their myths, treasuring and honoring them, finding truths about themselves in them. But they have assumed an archeological aspect: They are now more a matter of who a people once thought they were and told themselves they were and no longer who they truly were or who they truly are. They have, then, passed into the past: They are artifacts. After such moments, a people can no longer deploy their myths to distinguish themselves from others. All such efforts, if made, end in embarrassment. For myth can no longer serve as the basis of one's claim to exclusivity or privilege.

In history, the mark of these moments lies in the collective awareness of a community—a village or a nation, it does not matter. There is a shared sense of irreversible loss, of something that has been stripped away irrevocably. It matters not at all whether anyone is able to articulate this awareness. Something is simply gone and not to be retrieved. Sometimes the events prompting this process— Can we call it "de-mythologization?—occur gradually; history conveys its message over a period of some years or decades. But depending on events and circumstances, the process can be so instantaneous as to resist the term "process." It is closer to a revelation. This, for example, was the fate of the Japanese in 1945. And it was America's fate in 2001. For most Americans, there had not been much by way of a preparatory prelude.

September 11 marked the shockingly abrupt end of several centuries of thinking, feeling, hoping, and believing in a version of America and its place in the world that endured such that many generations could assume it to be eternally so. Surely this instantly severed assumption of eternal truth contributed to the complex of feelings Americans had that day—shock being but one among many. It was not the loss of life—not in the end—or the material loss in New York or Washington that knocked America off its feet. It was the loss of a scale of values that Americans had taken to be beyond the reach of anyone but the providential God.

To me, the efficacy of America's national myths seemed to have begun a gradual decline in April 1975. Americans then began to enter an era of exhaustion, of a flagging of the will—defeat by any other name. Every effort afterward to resuscitate the national myths, to retrieve their validity, simply ended up making the opposite of the intended point, for to manipulate myth, consciously to represent it, is implicitly to declare it to be myth and myth alone. This was Reagan's misunderstanding in the 1980s, and it would be George W. Bush's after 2001. These efforts do not survive the coming of history: They are ephemeral. And as September 11 marked the coming of history among us, it gave all alive that day a new kind of memory—a memory of indelible, ineffable loss—and a new kind of future, a future that hung in the balance, a future not yet determined, a future with nothing inevitable about it, a future that would require Americans to rotate their gaze and decide upon it.

———

Within three days of the attacks on New York and Washington, President George W. Bush had begun constructing a new national narrative—a way for Americans to understand and respond to what had happened to them. He needed something approximating a consensus: This would be essential if Washington was to execute its strategy. Bush needed a certain kind of American self, just as the Cold War's architects needed Cold War man. It would be a constructed self, a conjured identity, and it would be persuasive primarily to those who entered upon it.

To put this point another way, Bush's strategy required that September 11 be cast as the opening of another global conflict—a war without limit in space or time and one in which little account of international or even American law need be taken. Accordingly, Bush promised a kind of Old Testament vengeance and a choice for every nation that had numerous echoes in the past: You are either with us or with the terrorists. Curtailed liberties at home were in the offing, but the administration invoked a well-tried, if wholly false, equation: The price of security required such an exchange. Investors were urged to buy stock as a patriotic, antiterrorist gesture, and citizens should be consumers and shop as a matter of duty. This was how the "war on terror" would be fought on the home front. To suggest an idea of the spectacles to come, a Marine Corps soprano reopened the New York Stock Exchange on September 17, after a four-day hiatus in trading.

By September 20, American bombers were moving into position to begin attacks on Afghanistan, where bin Laden was believed to be taking sanctuary. The bombing began two weeks later. The coalition Bush had assembled was little more than unilateralism with a few token European participants. As planned, this was America's next war; after a decade of drift, it had found another mortal enemy at last. It was nothing so tangible as a nation; it was the shapeless thought of "terror," which made this war harder to define than any other America had entered upon.

But it was not so strange a war as it seemed at the time. The enemy was invisible and unknowable and without limit, but so, quite often, had the communists seemed. Democratic rights were to be withdrawn, but so had they been during the Cold War. Urging people to shop and vacation during so somber a passage in their history seemed risibly misjudged. But that, too, was how America fought the Cold War: fearful on the one hand, and on the other smiling and consuming. As a psychological construct, then, Bush's war was in essence a reprise, an act of nostalgia. And at this we cannot be surprised. America during the Bush administration stood on history's very cusp. This was the true source of the nation's unease. To go back and back and back again into the inventory of American images, like an actor inspecting his wardrobe closet—this was the best a president of Bush's beliefs and capacities could do. It would allow the American gaze to remain fixed upon the past, where better days awaited their return.

Among the many striking things about Bush's reaction to September 11 was how swiftly it elicited evidence of his religious fervor and his fidelity to the national myth. The term "evil" was deployed incessantly, as if it were a mantralike invocation. "The evil one" or "the evil ones" were favored references. At its extremes, the president's language proved worrisome—certainly overseas, and among some in Washington, too. "The great purpose of our great land," Bush declared two months after the attacks, "is to rid this world of evil and terror. The evil ones have roused a mighty nation, a mighty land."[2] America had returned to its historic mission, then, and Bush saw it in Manichean terms such that no one could know its limit. The *New York Times* quoted a close Washington acquaintance of the president's as saying, "I think, in his frame, this is what God has asked him to do."[3]

Much later, when he was recruiting other nations for the war in Iraq, Bush telephoned French President Jacques Chirac—twice, by reliable French accounts—and made reference to Gog and Magog, the satanic biblical figures found in Revelation, who appeared when the "end time" was near and the great war between good and evil was at last to be fought. This was how the American president was addressing foreign leaders in early 2003, unbeknownst to Americans. Chirac, it turned out, was so troubled by Bush's "state of mind" that he determined to keep these conversations secret until both he and Bush had left office. Accounts of the exchanges were published in France in 2009. They were unpublished in America until William Pfaff brought out *The Irony of American Destiny* in 2010.[4]

Bush used the word "hate" liberally during this time, and it crept inexorably into the newspapers and the national discourse. "They hate what they see right here in this chamber," Bush told a joint session of Congress a week after the attacks. "Their leaders are self-appointed. They hate our freedoms, our freedom of religion, our freedom of speech, our freedom to vote and assemble and disagree with one another."[5]

This was how the Bush administration constructed its narrative after September 11. There was a certain moral corruption in this endeavor—in the conscious act of making a useful story out of a tragedy and also in the narrative itself. In time, much of the country would partake of this corruption. Nothing at all need be said about anything at all America had ever done to other people. This could have nothing to do with the origins of the war on terror—a crucial distinction. Evil had befallen Americans because of their goodness, and they must avenge it, destroy it by way of a "crusade," in the certain knowledge that the providential hand guided them. "This is civilization's fight," Bush told Congress. "Freedom and fear are at war, and God is not neutral between them."

This is remarkable rhetoric, seventeenth century in vintage. Closer to our time, it is the fruit of the long, steady march of evangelical Christianity into the heart of Washington. Reagan signaled this with his talk of a religious revival. Bush brought it inside the White House gates—an advance that still bears abundant consequences in American political discourse. A few months before the

2008 election, Condoleezza Rice, Bush's secretary of state, advised Americans, "It is America's job to change the world, and in its own image."[6] It is faithful to the myth, but it would be difficult to think of a more radically wrong reading of America's moment at the time Rice wrote.

In this manner, Bush invited Americans into a world of infinite duty in the service of good and infinite terror in the doing of it. This, again, was not unlike the Cold War in either aspect. It was difficult to mistake the relish with which Bush assumed his new "role," as the *New York Times* liked to put it. He was a "war president," he grandly declared. This could give his administration shape and mission and the possibility of a new chapter in American heroism—all of which the Bush White House had lacked before September 11. In this way Bush's was to be a highly representational presidency: heroic as the presumed American victory in the Cold War was heroic, as 1945 was heroic, as Pearl Harbor was in its way heroic, and 1918 and 1898. And it is in its representational dimension that the newly declared war on terror would derive and deliver to Americans its largest meaning: The American century would go on. The price paid in lost "freedoms" would be high, but this was now America's crusade—a term Bush favored—and God, through the Oval Office, was with us as he always had been.

———

Many Americans, and maybe most, appeared to accept this swiftly made official narrative: a story not only of what had taken place and why but of how Americans were to feel and think and what they were to do about what had taken place. In a public opinion poll conducted in September 2001 by CBS, the broadcasting network, and the *New York Times,* ninety-two percent of respondents thought America should take military action against those responsible for the attacks. Seventy-nine percent said they were willing to accept losing some of their personal freedoms for the sake of national security.

But buried in this poll we find a suggestion of another thread of thinking. Seventy-eight percent of those questioned thought America should patiently determine who was responsible for the events of September 11 before retaliating. This compared with seventeen percent who said they wanted immediate action (as Bush was then planning) against all suspects. These polls were published on September 25, two weeks after the events.

———

"How do we respond to evil? What do we do for justice? Let it flow, the anger? Let it flow rampant? Or do we call for measures of reason, responsibility? Measures against the perpetrators? What do we do for prayers? And what do we do for peace? It is a time for questions. To sit with reflection. We must be extremely careful. And careful with ourselves. So it doesn't turn into resentment. We have many things to think about. Now we do this: Just sit together."[7]

These are the words of J. Rolando Matalon, a rabbi at the B'nai Jeshurun congregation in New York, spoken the Saturday after the September 11 attacks—at about the time CBS and the *Times* were gathering their polling data. They are laudable, these words. Sitting, a dozen years later, with a chronological collection of American newspapers of that time, it is easy to miss this side of American sentiment. What comes through all the newsprint is the remarkable fidelity of the American media to the officially structured universe of feeling and thought. Only with careful scrutiny (and memory) can one discover or recall the profound uncertainty and self-doubt Americans felt. This is a case of history without memory in the making, or perhaps the creation of an imaginary present—which comes to the same thing. But I recall that autumn well precisely as a "time for questions," a time "to sit with reflection," and it is for this that one may honor it as among the most interesting, dignified, and promising seasons in recent American history.

All that fall questions were raised and thoughts shared. With notable exceptions, there was a lessening of ideological fervor among Americans. The questions began with the most obvious: Why? What had we done? And to whom? And how long had we been doing it? Bin Laden, in the first of his occasional videos made public after the attacks, mentioned America's toleration of, if not collusion with, Israel in its treatment of Palestinians. Washington dismissed this out of hand. But was this truly so? Was there such a connection? Or—as bin Laden also suggested—did it have to do with American troops stationed in Saudi Arabia, the Islamic holy land? Was it broader than this? Did September 11 reflect a half-century of American prerogative in the Islamic world?

Bin Laden had a historicist's mind, to put it mildly; his references to wrongs, West to East, went back centuries. Among Americans, it was the present and the future that mattered. There was much talk of poverty and global iniquities. There was talk of how deprivation and poor schools and bad housing in the developing world hatched terrorists as pools of still water hatched insects. To address the question of terror we must address these things, the argument (also historicist) ran. The global North and South had to draw closer together. We must rededicate ourselves to the Millennium Development Goals, established in 2000. So far as I am able to recall, Americans had not looked out and considered the world in this fashion at any moment in my lifetime. Some, at least, and perhaps many, wanted to abandon the isolation America's power had brought upon it, so commencing new kinds of relations with the world.

With a billion children living in poverty, talk also arose of a Marshall Plan for the third world. Finance ministers and economists spoke of redeveloping our own societies such that we consumed less. "We have inescapable obligations beyond our front doors and garden gates," Gordon Brown, then England's chancellor of the exchequer, said before the New York Federal Reserve Bank not long after the attacks. "Thinking, not vengeance," a Washington research institution counseled. "World security depends on a creative reordering of spending priorities," two commentators reflected later in the *Boston Globe*. George Soros, the noted financier, put the point more technocratically a week after the attacks. "We need to create international mechanisms for the provision of public goods on a global scale," he asserted in a speech to the Asia Society. "This is the missing component in our current institutional arrangements."[8] What captivated me about the time I describe and all its questions was that it expressed an impulse to look toward the future with the thought that we were responsible for it.

There were, in keeping with the Marine band at the stock exchange, less thoughtful efforts to mark the September 11 events. What did they mean, these cryptic messages seeming to come from another place? They suggested a certain unexamined numbness. So often, they were written in the language of sentimentality, the language of feigned feeling, and so the language of no feeling. But we must count them as a piece of the mosaic that Americans made in the autumn of 2001.

In a Liz Claiborne window in midtown Manhattan:

Hope: Look to the future
with great expectations
lighting a holiday candle;

making a dull winter bright;

fulfilling the heart's desire;

wishing on a star;

believing in what's important.

Or this, in a shop along Fifth Avenue, with a silver border around it:

Peace:

inner contentment with

global harmony;

being at one with yourself;

uniting together for a common cause;

the serene simplicity of silence;

an undisturbed blanket of snow.

To understand these phrases, they are best taken as lists of things Americans could not have at that time: peace, hope, inner contentment, a certainty about the world. They were lists of longings, lists of what once was and would be no longer. They were expressions of sadness and loss, without meaning to be. And in their odd way they, too, were reflections of the great diversity of American sentiment in the post–September 11 period. How, then, can we still grasp—in a way that may never make the history books—what Americans were authentically thinking and feeling and wanting to do in response to the most shocking attack upon their nation in its history?

My interpretation of that time reflects the significance I assign to the September 11 attacks themselves. I have described that day as a collision with history. And in its aftermath we find a war of a certain kind—a domestic war that was partly one of words but also one of consciousness and symbols and affect. It was a war between those dedicated to sustaining sacred time and national myth and those attempting to think historically and place events in a historical context such that Americans could achieve an understanding of them. Beneath this, one can but guess as to the number of Americans who understood the magnitude of their moment.

Myth and history had contended for a century by September 11, 2001. Only twice before had this tension been so open and evident: There was 1898, on the eve of the war with Spain, and there was the Depression era of the 1930s. Only at these moments had history risen so close to the surface of American life and thought as it did in the autumn I describe. For a time, it seemed as if Americans were prepared at last to enter into that culture of defeat I have noted in an earlier essay.

It was an interesting display in many of its aspects, moving in a few. But the truly notable performance was the administration's. One cannot be certain, but all the evidence suggests that Bush believed, just as he suggested, in the magnitude of the moment as a kind of war-of-the-worlds conflict between absolute good and absolute evil. Those around the president, notably Vice President Cheney and Defense Secretary Donald Rumsfeld, suggest a more cynical conclusion. This divide—between those committed to American myth and those beyond it but finding it useful as a political and policy mechanism—had been evident in Washington for decades, at least since the Reagan years. It may be that the profundity of Bush's belief, with his near-paranoiac references to Gog and Magog and so on, was the perfect match for the calculating apparatchiks who surrounded the president and who appear to have made many of his decisions.

It is doubtful that anyone committed to "thinking with history," to borrow from the scholar Carl Schorske, thought at the time in such terms or understood all of what was at stake in this civil war for American minds. One recalls no one suggesting that two different ideas of what America was were in contention. But to take a great and tragic event and search for a way to invest it with meaning—to put it in context, in a word—this was true heroism. To seek causality in the affairs of one's nation is to accept risk—the risk, precisely, of uncovering causality in which one is implicated. It is to stand at history's threshold and allow oneself to be drawn across it. It is to recognize the condition of history without memory and then abandon it. There is a surrender involved, equally: As I have suggested in an earlier essay, it is a surrender of identities rooted in innocence, virtue, and omnipotence. Altogether, it involves a surrender of sacred time and myth, and from this there is no going back. This surrender, too, is heroic.

What interests me most, in hindsight, is how raw the terms of the national discourse were, how stripped of skin, but also how little understood. Myth and history: Who would have considered such apparent abstractions? There were those who sought to cultivate feelings—sorrow, anger, confusion, vengefulness—and preclude self-examination. And then there were those who wanted Americans to do just the opposite: Let us think this through. Let us think and ask questions. Let us reflect. This was the defining divide of the time, and in this I have no doubt that Rabbi Matalon was a man of history.

———

Sometime in the 1960s or seventies, the sensation of living without an organic attachment to history began to catch up to some Americans. It was possibly the same as in the 1890s, when the context the past supplies to life seemed to fade into the distance, beyond one's grasp. In the sixties and seventies, this seemed related to the progressive privatization in American life, a Cold War consequence. In 1980 the writer George Trow published a noted essay on this phenomenon in the *New Yorker*. He called it "Within the Context of No Context," and he focused primarily on television. Television flattened consciousness, he suggested—consciousness and temporality. "Television is the frame of no-history, and it holds the archives of the history of no-history."[9]

Life without any social or cultural context had (and has) a political dimension to it. Trow was describing another aspect of Cold War man. And it lingers among us, as became clear in American thinking in the autumn of 2001. The war of thought I have described was fought between those who would view the events of September 11 in a proper context and those who, led by the administration, actively sought to discourage such a view. One of the notable aspects of an ideology, it has been remarked, is its power to suppress unwanted inquiry. This was part of what impoverished Cold War man. In our time, it is part of what sustains the construct of the sayable and the unsayable. In 2001, then, it was thought or the confinement of thought. As from the nation's very beginning, the patriotic way was to turn to emotion to interpret the world, rather than thought. Feeling American was quite sufficient, the desired thing.

The most interesting and outspoken of those opposed to the kind of thought one would assume to be logical was named Richard Perle. A longtime political consultant in the capital's conservative circles, Perle was a member of the Pentagon's Defense Policy Board in 2001. And he had already coined the term for which he became noted when the attacks of September 11 occurred. "We must decontextualize terrorism," Perle said on repeated occasions. "Any attempt to discuss the roots of terrorism is an attempt to justify it. It simply needs to be fought and destroyed."[10]

Many unworthy things passed for sensible thought that autumn. Such was the nation's stunned confusion; America was on wholly unfamiliar ground—the ground of history. But few ideas articulated that season appear in hindsight to be so ignorant and damaging. If there was any moment when the nation needed an understanding of the wide, becoming world beyond its borders, it was then. If there was any moment when America needed to come to terms with terrorism's roots and causes, was it not also then?

Perle had already used his dressed-up term in the context of Israel and the Palestinians. There is no need to understand why Palestinians resist occupation of their land, he asserted. It is a yet more preposterous application of the thought: No need for history, no need for politics, no need for an understanding of geography, of what had happened. In both cases, Perle did much to confine America's awareness, as if to protect it, from any constructive expansion. He was flattening the picture, as television does. In so doing, he also did much to mold the identification of terror and Islam in many American minds. This is a tragedy Americans still live with.

To see things in such a way is the consequence of living in that isolated, desolate present Nietzsche described, between the high hedges of past and future. As Trow would put it, Americans were therefore unable to understand the meaning and worth of context. This renders a people into a state of perverse innocence, a frightening innocence, as one finds in Huxley's *Brave New World,* wherein history is not taught and history books are forbidden.

This condition is disturbingly similar to America's. As I write these sentences, Perle's thought of "decontextualizing" terror is posted on the Web site of the Homeland Security Department, as if it were a kind of guiding truth.[11]

————

Individuality has been a running theme in American discourse since the nineteenth century, when it was elevated to one of the nation's exceptional attributes. It is noted in romanticized visions of the West once explorers, fur traders, adventurers, and the like crossed the great rivers in the middle of the country and began traversing the Great Plains. The iconography of myth took hold very early. By 1870 or so, Buffalo Bill Cody was traveling the East with a successful "Wild

West" show—knowing full well that easterners had not the faintest idea as to genuine life on the frontier. It was possibly America's first reenactment. Even then, the fronticrsman as totemic individual had taken hold in imaginations "back East."[12]

We should consider this tradition of imagery and self-portraiture briefly. It bears upon how Americans portrayed themselves to themselves after the events of 2001.

Among the first to depict Americans in the American West were painters. They began to make expeditions, often with a wealthy patron, in the 1830s—decades before Buffalo Bill Cody or Frederic Remington would make their contributions to the myth of the self-reliant western man. One of these early painters was named Alfred Jacob Miller. A native of Baltimore, he had studied for two years in France before setting up a studio in New Orleans. It was there in 1837 a Scot named Sir William Drummond Stewart engaged Miller to accompany him on a westward expedition to provide picturesque scenes of the landscapes and figures they would encounter.

Miller did well. He captured lone fur trappers, Native Americans, and reckless gallops across stony streams. But the collection Miller produced never earned the attention that the work of other painters did. Much of it hung in Stewart's castle; the rest remained in Miller's family in Baltimore and was rarely placed on exhibition.

Miller's obscurity lasted a century, for in the 1940s the fortunes of his work took a turn. A collector in Kansas City brought the pictures to the attention of Bernard DeVoto, the noted writer. DeVoto was then writing *Across the Wide Missouri* and took to Miller's paintings immediately, finding in them the embodiment of the mountain men, hunters, and trappers he was writing about. When DeVoto published *Wide Missouri* in 1947, it included numerous of Miller's paintings—nearly a hundred. DeVoto, who was born in Utah, saw in Miller's pieces (and wrote into his text) a model for the post–World War II American character. Miller's figures never quit, never gave in, always insisted that they would live or die on their own terms. Life was an act of conscious will, and DeVoto found it precisely where Frederick Jackson Turner had in 1893: on the frontier, the raw western edge of America.[13]

Miller's story has an odd shape to it, given that it somewhat serendipitously involves one of the mid-twentieth century's most admired writers. But from Miller to DeVoto there is a visible line of transmission. Between them, one sees how the myth of American individuality passes through the decades—in this case nearly intact. One also sees how the prevailing idea of the American individual was essential to the way the nation conducted itself during the American century. DeVoto wrote just as the Cold War was taking shape. Americans needed to summon their true character if they were to prevail, he considered; he intended to suggest this in *Across the Wide Missouri*. One finds something of the same in 2001 and the years that followed: So much of what was said and done then was dedicated to a cultivation of the heroic in American terms.

There was much talk among young people about joining the military to fight in Afghanistan, for instance. (Iraq was still two years away.) And many young men and women did volunteer, sometimes making considerable changes in their lives. Interesting moments occurred. Just why were people enlisting and what were they thinking? How did they understand America's predicament at that moment? Were they captives of myth? Was the war on Afghanistan another representation? On a national radio program late in September, several young men and women discussed these matters and considered the army as a career. One of them cautiously introduced the thought that Americans should perhaps look at the world with better understanding and begin to ask questions.

My journal for that day indicates that the program's host pounced with a smothering riposte. "Four American passenger jets were hijacked, three flown into American buildings, thousands of lives are lost, and we are supposed to ask what we did wrong?" He feigned incredulity.

This is how Richard Perle's "decontextualization" came to be applied. One of the bequests that comes to us from the nineteenth century is a feature of the individual one finds nowhere else. Action is quite consistently favored over thought or consideration. The latter two, indeed, are somewhat suspect. Heroic Americans, then, are heroic for their deeds, not their thoughts or ideas: They act, they assert their wills, according to mythologically derived identities. Recall Dewey's advocacy of action over ideals in *The Quest for Certainty*. This is the consciousness out of which he wrote.

For much of the autumn of 2001 the *New York Times* carried a daily section called A Nation Challenged. It included war news, diplomatic news, reports from the Pentagon, stories about "jittery Americans." On September 23 it reported that Texas had reinstituted prayer in its public schools in defiance of a Supreme Court ruling a year earlier. The *Times* cited the Bush administration's ostentatious resort to prayer after September 11. It was God and science to which Americans were supposed to turn that autumn.

After a time, much of public life in America was drained through the sieve of September 11. New York determined to take up a gambling bill that had lain fallow for years: The state needed to make up for economic losses caused by the attacks. All was different now: Bush's tax cuts, missile defense, trade negotiating authority—all of this was seen in another light. What is so striking as one wades again through a season's newspapers is the paucity of new thinking as the autumn went on. Few of the ideas that appeared briefly to blossom after September 11 were reflected in the nation's direction. There was little evidence of anything one would call original or imaginative. Faced with the wholly new and unexpected, Americans' response fell startlingly short of the occasion. Our days as makers, as constructors, seemed to be over. We lived on what had already been made, and we longed only to return to old habits.

One of the interesting features of the *Times*'s section, A Nation Challenged, was a page each day headlined "Portraits in Grief." It consisted of a dozen or more thumbnail photographs of those killed at the World Trade Center, each one accompanied by a few paragraphs on the deceased.

The *Times* called the portraits "glimpses of lives," or "glimpses of victims." Here are two, chosen at random:

Carl Flickinger: Golf, Gadgets and Gifts Carl Flickinger considered his work hours at Cantor Fitzgerald to be one of the job's biggest benefits. Though he started at 7 a.m., he was home by 6:30 p.m. with his family in Congers in Rockland County.

Mr. Flickinger, 38, slid comfortably into domestic routines. Every Saturday, he shopped for groceries before taking his 11-year-old twin sons to the mall for sneakers and jeans. In the evening he checked his sons' homework and read to his 5-year-old daughter. On and off the job he drove himself. He would not just play an easy 18 holes of golf—he took lessons and practiced on the driving range.

Mr. Flickinger was a gadget guy, said his wife, Kathy, and he liked to buy the latest nifty devices as gifts for friends. Every morning before his commute, he bought coffee at the Dairy Mart and left it for his wife. And at 11 a.m., he always called home. "Just to touch base," she said. "Just to tell me how his morning was going."[14]

That is from the *Times*'s September 28 edition. This was carried on October 9:

George Bishop: A Cliché, but Accurate Do not tell Betsy Bishop that the description "Family Man" is a cliché—she knows it. Still, there is no better way to characterize her husband, George Bishop, who, she said, treasured taking his two sons to soccer games, going to beach vacations, having guests for intimate dinners and listening to music.

"He wouldn't just have music on in the background, he'd *really* be listening to it," Mrs. Bishop said. "And he wasn't a party person, but he was a very genial host, great at bringing people together."

Mr. Bishop, who was 52 and worked for the Aon Corporation, was the kind of person who could bring you your papers on the way back from the office fax machine, or walk a seeing-eye dog three miles a day as a favor, just to give it exercise.[15]

"Portraits in Grief" ran regularly for many weeks. Who were the people depicted in those pages, one began to wonder. "Mr. Wilson always spoke to the fish when he returned home, his daughter said." "Samantha and George were just about to buy their first apartment." What did such details mean? These items were not obituaries. What purpose did they serve?

I saved all the "Portraits," curious about them in a way I did not understand but intuiting that I might one day write about them. It took a long time to interpret them. It occurred to me at one point that those portrayed were the last to live and die in the American century, with all its illusions and presumptions. This is so, I think, and a useful way to think of them. At the time, in 2001, all I knew was that somehow the "Portraits in Grief" offended me.

I eventually began to think of Alfred Jacob Miller's paintings and the customary portrayal of people who painted in Miller's genre. When Miller depicted a figure, he painted a kind of radical individualist, often against a vast, forbidding, unpopulated background. One finds, for instance, a fur trapper and his pack horse against the backdrop of an immense mountain range beyond the reach of humanity. Individuality: Everyone who died at the World Trade Center had to be established as an individual. This individuation had to be accomplished in ordinary, somewhat unthinking ways, devoid of politics or much of a public life, for they had to be framed without a knowable, discernible context. They stared out from the newspaper's pages from a different place—from sacred time and sacred space, just as the figures in Miller's paintings did. Each of the portraits, without fail, featured a kind of ostentatious normality in the life of its subject. In every one there was the kind of compulsory happiness one found in Cold War man.

They were also innocent, the tragic victims of the World Trade Center attacks. This attribute was key. For if America was going to respond cleanly and clearly and without ambiguity to a wrong committed against it, the nation and all in it would have to be innocent. And by this I mean not merely innocent of provoking the attacks in any direct way, but innocent for all time. The World Trade Center victims were innocent for all of us, then. This was the point of "decontextualization"—or one of them. It was the point of the radio host who scoffed at the idea of thinking through the prior events that may have precipitated September 11 as a response. Decontextualization precludes not only an examination of others; more significantly, it precludes self-examination. That is why the "Portraits in Grief" are filled with so many pedestrian details—golf balls, goldfish, electronic gadgets—but do not add up in any case to even the promised glimpse of an authentic existence. No one in them bears any responsibility for anything outside of his or her private life.

Over time I concluded that the "Portraits," if only obliquely, reflected something of the nature of life and death during the American century. Those in them lived in mythological time. There was the desire to salvage the victims from anonymity. All were to be named and honored. This is quite understandable. But it is so only against a certain background. This background stands as vast and silent and distant as a mountain range in one of Miller's paintings, and it is populated with the millions of unnamed and unknown others who perished as a consequence of American ambition. All Americans stand against this background. It is a mode of seeing. I have already noted that I was unwilling to mourn the dead of the World Trade Center. It was because I could not participate in the ritual of inno- cence; I could not erase the background against which all Americans live and lose their lives.

To see only the individuals in the foreground is to see with a mythologically defined consciousness—without context. To see the picture as a whole is to see with a historically educated eye, to see oneself in the context of one's life, one's world, and what has made these as they are.

———

"None of us would ever wish the evil that was done on Septem- ber the 11th. Yet after America was attacked, it was as if our entire country looked into a mirror and saw our better selves. We were reminded that we are citizens, with obligations to each other, to our country, and to history. We began to think less of the goods we can accumulate, and more about the good we can do."[16]

It is not a bad description of the autumn of 2001, even if it is short on detail. Americans did begin to behold themselves as if in a mirror—the most courageous thing they could do, for it had been many years since they had considered who they were with scru- tiny as against narcissistic self-regard. But the speech from which I have drawn did not, ironically, encourage the sort of national self- examination the passage suggests. It is a portion of George W. Bush's first State of the Union address, delivered on January 29, 2002. Read properly, that speech was calculated to set the new national mood in place, pushing all the questioning of the autumn into the forgotten past and declaring a new course based on aggressive action.

There are many things to say about Bush's "Axis of Evil" speech, as it is known. Certainly it was intended in part to "scare hell out of the American people," as a senator famously counseled President Truman while he prepared to ask the nation for many extra billions of dollars to finance the new national security state. Hence, terrorists were to be counted in the tens of thousands; Al Qaeda was active in at least a dozen countries. The defense budget was to be increased by its largest increment in twenty years. "These enemies view the entire world as a battlefield, and we must pursue them wherever they are," Bush told Americans that evening. "So long as training camps operate, so long as nations harbor terrorists, freedom is at risk. And America and our allies must not, and will not, allow it."

All that followed during Bush's two terms in office—the war in Iraq, Guantánamo Bay, "extraordinary renditions," the Patriot Act—was prefigured in that speech. We have obligations to history, Bush had said. But reading the speech again now, many years later, it seems to me the president merely felt obliged to make such a reference so as to connect with the mood of the country. The unusual force of the speech was intended to counter this mood. Bush's true purpose in his "Axis of Evil" speech was to close the door on the autumn's givenness to self-examination. As I recall that time, it seems to me now that Bush was simply trying to draw a line under that reflective mood and continue constructing another national mood, within which there would be no place for reflection.

This mood would draw Americans firmly back into their national myths. Once again, everything had changed on September 11, but at bottom nothing was different. America was still America, just as it always had been—exceptional, impregnable against the blows of history. America's way forth would rest on power, prerogative, and aggressive action. This time the enemy was "evil" itself, which resided (in its abstract fashion) everywhere. America's task, then, would be long and without limit: Bush said this much in his January 29 speech. As much or more than during the Cold War years, America became once again more reliant than at any other time in history on military power, or the threat of it.

In the autumn of 2004, Karl Rove, Bush's noted political strategist, said something remarkable to a journalist questioning him about the administration's foreign and military policies. By this time the war in Iraq had begun, the war in Afghanistan was grinding on, and "the war president" was about to be elected to a second term. The published passage concerning Rove, who is named only as "the aide," deserves to be quoted at length:

> The aide said that guys like me were "in what we call the reality-based community," which he defined as people "who believe that solutions emerge from your judicious study of discernible reality. . . ." "That's not the way the world works anymore," he continued. "We're an empire now, and when we act, we create our own reality. And while you're studying that reality—judiciously, as you will—we'll act again, creating other new realities, which you can study, too. And that's how things will sort out. We're history's actors . . . and you, all of you, will be left just to study what we do."[17]

This was an astonishing monument to the time. It was at once among the most extraordinary claims an American had ever made to an exemption from history and a frightening admission of the recklessness that had characterized so much of the American century.

Rove's thought had a long history. Were Americans not intent on creating a new world from the nation's founding? Closer to our time, did not Truman and Eisenhower share the same ambition? The remarkable aspect of Rove's thinking is how fully and faithfully it was grounded in American myth. This was the essence of the Bush years. And in Rove's declaration we find something that was to become familiar among conservatives: We find desperation, a rejection of reality itself born of the terror that comes with standing at history's edge.

The immediacy of power as its own self-justifying argument: This is what the Bush years finally represented. America fought two wars as a consequence. Each had something in common with the Spanish-American War—a display of power for the display's sake, the demonstration of unlimited prerogative and impunity. Consider the dead—the truly innocent dead: at least 118,000 civilians in Iraq, and probably more; 12,000 to 15,000 in Afghanistan up to mid-2011.[18] These died, along with combatants, so that America could preserve the illusion that its century was not over.

A friend once recalled in conversation that she remembered the seven years that followed September 11 "the way one does a bad movie." The analogy is useful. Time was again transformed during those years, as it is in films. On each occasion one encountered an armed soldier at a rail station or an airport, one was reminded that life in America had begun to unfold in the militarized time of permanent surveillance. This is also to say self-surveillance: "If you see something, say something," we are still incessantly urged. September 11 announced a world requiring our attention, certainly. But it did not justify (and has not yet justified) the transformation of our national political life: We were a nation at war, we were told, but war turned out to be a kind of metaphor, shorthand for all that went into the claim of American prerogative. At home, one was invited simply to watch—silently, as in a cinema. All had become spectacle, pure allegory—which is to say, pure representation. And, as representation always does, it fixed the gaze backward, leaving Americans blind even to the present.

——

One Christmas morning when I was very small, we five—my father and mother and sister and brother and I—gathered in our living room to see what Santa Claus had left under our tree. Soon enough, the object of our very immense excitement was a Polaroid instant camera.

I recall the scene vividly. We were in a house that put us somewhere in the mid-1950s. Eisenhower would have been president, and the disgrace of Senator Joseph McCarthy would not have been far behind us. But we were innocent of such things. We gave the world as it truly was little conscious thought. I remember my father's large, guileless smile and our shared anticipation. I remember the elegant leather case the camera came in—well-finished, well-stitched, as if it would be a thing passed down from one generation to the next like a fine pair of old binoculars or a beautifully crafted whiskey flask.

In those days one had to smear each Polaroid image with a stick of gluelike substance—presumably a photographic fixer of some kind. I recall so well that pink, pungent grease as we puzzled over it. We made our first pictures that morning, of course. It was as if we could not wait to see ourselves in those images that somehow transformed us.

The Polaroid sensation did not last long in our family. Soon enough the camera and its case and the box both came in took their place on the hat shelf in the hall closet—that small zone of lost enthusiasms. It rarely came out again, so far as I am able to remember. The images were very small in those early days of instant photography, and there are very few in the flotsam of our family's stream.

All this came back to me one morning in the autumn of 2001. It was October. I had gone out to the barn to look for a set of files, and there at the bottom of the wrong box was the Polaroid. I took it out: The case and the camera in it were in immaculate condition. Only the box showed any wear: Plainly it had shuffled from household to household for decades and had at last landed in mine. The week before this discovery, on October 11, Polaroid had declared bankruptcy. I had not taken any notice at the time, but, holding the camera in my hands—perfect and perfectly useless all at once—it seemed to betoken the end of an era, at least in the way of personal history.

Years later, what had become of the old Polaroid caused me to reflect. I considered the ways Americans saw and did not see themselves. Did Americans, then as now, truly desire to see themselves? It seemed a germane question. Did we not harbor a truer desire to hide from ourselves and all that we had made of ourselves, for there was so very much to hide (and hide from) if we were to maintain our smiles and our innocence? We had no such thoughts at the time, of course. These came later. The Polaroid became for me a kind of signifier of a certain time, a lost time. Why did it disappear so quickly into our place of lapsed enthusiasms? It was as if we were enticed by this fashionable product to see ourselves in images technology could give us, but also, as if we were a primitive tribe, we somehow feared its power to portray us just as we were.

What was it we—most of us, in any case—purported to be innocent of in those days? Our conduct of the Cold War, certainly, both abroad and at home. But there was something more. How little did most of us understand technology and what it would produce. How greatly did we trust in it. The mid-1950s seems late for an innocence of this kind to linger. But we knew nothing of the power technology would cast over us, nothing of the confusion it would create between means and ends, nothing of the speed with which it would move and change, or the damage that speed would wreak upon our consciousness. None of this was even remotely apparent to us back then—not to us and not, it seems to me, to any but a very few of those in control of our technological advances.

I recount these memories—the deep memory of a Christmas long ago and the more recent memory of finding the camera—because a certain recognition arose from them. Among the startling things about the time I have recalled, the mid-1950s, is how remote it is now. We can draw nothing from the people I describe. Their time is distant the way World War II became quickly distant during the fifties. "History is accelerating," a French writer named Daniel Halévy observed just after the war.[19] We are living what he meant. Our dividing line now is 2001. Were we not shocked that year in part by the sensation of seeing ourselves at last—ourselves and ourselves among others? Many of us have said, at one time or another, that we live in a world we were not brought up to live in. This is true now of the nation. It is also part of what Halévy meant. America, ever dedicated to its original design, is not a nation made for this time. It has always had a past—Hegel's remark in 1826 notwithstanding. And now we must be especially attentive to it. We must reinvolve ourselves with it. We must look again at all the old images and find ourselves in them as we truly were, not as we thought we were at the time. I say this not for the sake of going back to the past—it is gone, of course, and that project is always folly—but for the sake of moving forward, moving on from where we once were and where we think we are now. This is our most pressing twenty-first-century task.

———

Myths enclose those who believe in them. They are not subject to debate or rational consideration. One cannot hold them up to the light and parse them for their true and applicable aspects as against their false and misleading ones. They are there, stories whose frequent telling has inscribed upon them a balanced, inalterable structure. This gives mythology its enclosing character. One lives either within it or not, one either accepts it as a guide to "what happened" or not and, finally, "what will happen." Questions of "self and other" arise, questions of intimacy and understanding or of distance and misunderstanding. Perceptions of self and other are often rooted in myths. And so it is for Americans.

I have called our time a time of demythologizing. It means simply that Americans are called upon now to advance beyond the mythologies that carried them from their nation's very beginnings until 2001, the opening of a new century. This makes our moment historically large, as large as the moments when our myths were first articulated almost four hundred years ago. For some, this point will not be difficult to grasp. Some or many Americans understand already, it seems to me, what truly happened in September 2001. But for others the point may prove nearly impossible to accept. We have all seen how the Bush administration represented the events of September 11 as a call to arms, a time to reaffirm the very things that, in those horrific moments, finally became untenable.

When we observe what we call our "culture wars," when we listen to our national political discourse, when we are asked to consider policies such as nationalized health care, or immigration, or the teaching of creationism in schools, or regulation in our markets, it is this, I think, we are truly holding up to ourselves. It is the question of myth or history: Do we claim still to live in sacred time, immune to change, our institutions providentially blessed just as they are, or have conditions at home and abroad advanced such that America, too, must advance—which is to say evolve historically and leave certain beliefs and practices behind? The question, to say nothing of any answers, seems nearly intractable. Too few of us seem able to face it. This accounts for the very unworkable condition of our national politics, for it represents an uncrossable divide. It is the "within" and "without" of myths that is at work. "In the end we couldn't connect," House Speaker John Boehner, a conservative Republican, said as he emerged from talks with President Obama in the summer of 2011. "Not because of different personalities, but because of different versions of our country." This is the point precisely.

Can a people disabuse themselves of their mythological beliefs? Emphatically they can, for there are examples threaded through history: the English, the Spanish, the Portuguese, the Germans, the Japanese, certainly the Chinese. All of these peoples and many others have let go of the national myths that had once driven them on. They may linger as stories that are understood to be no more than that. But that is all. In every case the change occurred as a response—to defeat, decolonization, internal decay, and sometimes more than one of these in combination. The dis-illusioning of a myth-driven people is always a national reply to the knock of history.

———

Do Americans want a future that is different from the present or the past? This question is key. To put it another way, is it possible for Americans to maintain a self-respectful notion of national identity within a new, dis-illusioned history of themselves? Can Americans remember differently—and therefore advance differently, without the nationalist and exceptionalist identity that carried them to 2001?

We have little to go by, and what we have is not encouraging. The Bush years amounted to a simple denial of historical facts, a life-wasting, resource-wasting lunge for what had already slipped away. The Obama presidency, for all its promise of change, has offered little in the way of movement. Barack Obama has clung to the same prerogative rights to conduct military action wherever he sees fit. His administration is guilty of many of the same abuses of law that characterized the Bush years. Apply a blind, and one cannot tell the difference between the security-related legislation Obama has passed and what Bush enacted from the Patriot Act onward. Does this reflect the standard liberal effort to mollify conservative adversaries on all questions related to defense? Does it signify some frightening, invisible hold the defense and intelligence establishments have over our political life? One suspects that Obama's heart has not been in some of what he has done overseas, but one cannot tell. The Cold War made our government unknowable in such respects. It took Bush two years after September 11 to turn the world's near universal sympathy into a degree of resentment or contempt unknown in American history. Obama has improved matters, but to nothing like the extent he could have. It is the same at home. One still finds little that differs from the fundamentalist beliefs that Americans have long held as to the markets, the government, and the individual in society.

Despite numerous appearances and encouragements, this is not the hour for pessimism. To seek affirmative answers to the questions I pose, even as we are unsure there are any, is the work of our time. I do not believe that America's decline is inevitable, the many signs that it has begun notwithstanding. Relative decline—decline in relation to rising powers—yes, the world is changing and this cannot be altered. We live in a new and different age, in which the positions of East and West and North and South are shifting fundamentally. Nor should Americans regret this: To bear less responsibility in the twenty-first century will do America good, just as the responsibilities it bore in the twentieth so often did not become it and proved a nearly ruinous burden. What is at issue, rather, is absolute decline, and this is America's to accept or counter.

If we are to take up this task, why must we begin with history? Why do good historians always insist on this? What does the past have to do with making a new future for ourselves? These questions will especially vex Americans, whom I have already placed among the world's great forgetters. To leave the past untouched, assuming it is fine just as it is, would doom Americans to more of it, as the old adage goes. Instead we must stir it, poke it as one does a fading fire. We must disturb it until we find ourselves in it as we truly are. We have not attempted this discovery yet. And we seem to be of two minds about the attempt.

Let us consider two ways Americans have of remembering. Each bears upon the post-2001 challenge Americans now struggle to address.

———

Just before and continuing after the September 11 attacks, an unusually public interest arose in the institution of slavery in the United States. Books and articles appeared about Jefferson's intimate relations with Sally Hemings, one of his slaves. A barn used to imprison slaves as they were force-marched westward was discovered and preserved in rural Kentucky. The *Hartford Courant,* after exposing the complicity of the city's insurers in financing and indemnifying the chattel of slaveowners, turned on itself to expose its own profits (via advertising) from the slave trade. Yale University acknowledged that it had financed scholarships, professorships, and its library with slaveowners' money.

There was much talk of reparations. A professor in New York reckoned, by way of an intricate set of historical and contemporary statistical data, that each black family in America should receive an average of thirty-five thousand dollars. A Yale professor named David Brion Davis offered this reflection on the Civil War and its aftermath:

The United States is only now beginning to recover from the Confederacy's ideological victory following the Civil War.

Though the South lost all the battles, for more than a century it attained its goal: that the role of slavery in American history be thoroughly diminished, even somehow removed as a cause of the war. The reconstitution of North and South required a national repudiation of Reconstruction as "a disastrous mistake"; a wide-ranging white acceptance of "Negro inferiority" and white supremacy in the South; and a disinterested view of slavery as an unfortunate but benign institution that was damaging for whites morally but helped civilize and Christianize "African savages."[20]

Judging by the proximity of the dates of this material, the question of slavery and responsibility captured a place and lingered in the public mind for about five years. I do not know why. The question of reparations now seems off-balance—ill-considered and, in any case, impractical. In historical situations of this kind, there is guilt and there is responsibility. Germans alive today are responsible for their nation's past (and almost always bear this responsibility with dignity and grace). But they are not guilty: The guilty are nearly all gone now. One cannot inherit guilt as if it were handed down from one generation to the next. It is responsibility one inherits, and to which one must attend. It is the same in the case of American slavery. White Americans are responsible for it and its consequences and should hold themselves so. But they are not guilty.

This point aside, the slavery debate that irrupted through the surface of American life a dozen or so years ago was highly constructive. It was history shared. It suggested that Americans are indeed capable of looking back and realizing a historical self-consciousness that alters their understanding of their past—and hence their present and future—while making some initial sense of the otherwise fraught pronoun "we." "We" very often denotes the mythological "we" of America—a "we" that does not exist. Here one finds a case in which it can be used with justification.

The period I recount gives us an idea of what Americans can do if they make up their minds that something is worth doing. The same can be said of the problem I have named history without memory: For a few square feet of the American past, history is no longer hollow. We know better now who we are, for we have made an investment in history. We live in historical time now, at least in the context of American slavery. The myths David Brion Davis enumerated are dead. In matters of race a true reexamination of historical reality has begun. And the possibilities this opens to us have already begun to arrive. In February 2012, President Obama broke ground at the Smithsonian Institution's latest project: the National Museum of African American History and Culture.

———

Now let us consider another kind of remembering in America. It is very different from the remembering Americans have managed to do by way of slavery—and it is very prevalent as a kind of national habit.

At one end of the Reflecting Pool in Washington, D.C., in the expanse between the Washington Monument and the Lincoln Memorial, the Bush administration authorized a memorial to World War II. This was a matter of months before the events of September 11. It seemed a strange design when it was first shown in the early summer of 2001, and so it proved when the monument was finished and open to the public in 2004.[21] It consists of fifty-six granite pillars arranged in two half-circles around a pool, each pillar standing for a state or territory, each endowed with a bronze wreath. Each side of the entranceway—graceful granite steps down to the level of the pool—is lined with a dozen bas-relief bronzes depicting important moments in either the European or the Pacific war: Here is the farm family gathered around the radio listening to Roosevelt announce America's declaration of war; here is a recruitment hall; here is a troop ship leaving harbor; here is a beach landing, there jungle warfare, and there helmets atop rifles honoring the fallen. At the opposite end of the small circular pool, a "freedom wall" commemorates the 400,000 American dead with 4,000 gold stars.

This message, chiseled into a stone tablet, greets the visitor to the World War II Memorial:

> Here in the presence of Washington and Lincoln,
> one the eighteenth-century father and the other
> the nineteenth-century preserver of our nation,
> we honor those twentieth-century Americans
> who took up the struggle during the Second World
> War and made the sacrifices to perpetuate the gift
> our forefathers entrusted to us, a nation conceived
> in liberty and justice.

One must spend a certain time at the memorial to grasp the message it is conveying. This has to do with the monument's style, as the bas-relief bronzes and the welcoming inscription suggest. This is not a memorial built by people of the early twenty-first century. Part of its purpose, indeed, is to erase all that Americans did between 1945 and 2001 so that we might insert ourselves into the morally pure era (supposedly, as we have reimagined it) of the Second World War. It functions, then, a little like Williamsburg or Sturbridge Village: It is history that is not-history, or not-history dressed up as history. It is history, in short, for those who are devoid of memory. The architect—Friedrich St. Florian, whose studio is in Rhode Island—accomplished this by designing in the style sometimes called modern classical. The modern classical style was popular in the 1930s and

forties. It is characterized by mass and volume in its forms and simplified articulations of minimal detail. Roosevelt might have built in
this style, as Stalin or Mussolini might have.

St. Florian's project, then, is a monument to forgetting, not remembering. There is no bas-relief dedicated to the atomic bomb attacks on Japan or the fire-bombings in Germany; all that occurred
after 1945 disappears into the memorial's antiquated style. We have
a hint of this if we consider the date of its conception and construction. The first decade of our new century was marked by a strong,
quite evident nostalgia for the Second World War. One found it
in best-selling books (*The Greatest Generation*) and in popular films
(*Pearl Harbor, Schindler's List*). The monument is of a piece with
these cultural productions. It is a memorial as we imagine such a
thing would have been made at the time being memorialized. It is a
reenactment of a sorrow that is beyond us to feel now. One cannot
say this about the other monuments ranged around the Reflecting
Pool. They are not reenactments; they are not in quotation marks.
In this case, one is placed back in the 1940s so as to see the forties.
It is history for people who cannot connect with history. Nostalgia
is always an expression of unhappiness with the present, and never
does it give an accurate accounting of the past. What are we to say
about a monument to a nostalgia for nostalgia?

———

The various symptoms of America's dysfunctional relationship with
its past are all in evidence in the Tea Party, the political movement
formed in 2009 and named for the Boston Tea Party of 1773. It
would be remiss not to note this. Much has been written about the
Tea Party's political positions: Its members are radically opposed to
taxation and favor a fundamentalist idea of the infallibility of markets
and an almost sacramental interpretation of the Constitution. They
cannot separate religion from politics, and they consider President

Obama either a socialist or a Nazi or (somehow) both. They hold to a notion of the individual that the grizzliest fur trapper west of the Missouri River 170 years ago would have found extreme. When the Tea Party first began to gather national attention, many considered it a caricature of the conservative position that held too distorted an idea of American history to last any consequential amount of time. Plainly this has been wrong, at least so far, given the number of seats the movement won in the legislative elections of November 2010: At this writing, they number sixty-two in the House of Representatives.

"Take our country back" is among the Tea Party's more familiar anthems. And among skeptics it is often asked, "Back to what?" I have heard various answers. Back to the 1950s is one, and this is plausible enough, given the trace of the movement's bloodlines back to the John Birch Society and others among the rabidly anticommunist groups active during the Cold War's first decade. But the answer I prefer is the eighteenth century—or, rather, an imaginary version of the eighteenth century. A clue to the collective psychology emerged in the movement's early days, when adherents dressed in tricorn hats, knee breeches, and brass-buckled shoes. This goes to the true meaning of the movement and explains why it appeared when it did. One cannot miss, in the movement's thinking and rhetoric, a desire for a mythical return, another "beginning again," a ritual purification, another regeneration for humanity.

Whatever the Tea Party's unconscious motivations and meanings—and I count these significant to an understanding of the group—we can no longer make light of its political influence; it has shifted the entire national conversation rightward—and to an extent backward, indeed. But more fundamentally than this, the movement reveals the strong grip of myth on many Americans—the grip of myth and the fear of change and history. In this, it seems to me, the Tea Party speaks for something more than itself. It is the culmination of the rise in conservatism we can easily trace to the 1980s. What of this conservatism, then? Ever since Reagan's "Morning in America" campaign slogan in 1984 it has purported to express a new optimism about America. But in the Tea Party we discover the true topic to be the absence of optimism and the conviction that new ideas are impossible. Its object is simply to maintain a belief in belief and an optimism about optimism. These are desperate endeavors. They amount to more expressions of America's terror in the face of history. To take our country back: Back to its mythological understanding of itself before the birth of its own history is the plainest answer of all.

I do not see that America has any choice now but to face this long terror. America's founding was unfortunate in the fear and apprehension it engendered, and unfortunate habits and impulses have arisen from it. These are now in need of change—a project of historical proportion. Can we live without our culture of representation, our images and symbols and allusions and references, so casting our gaze forward, not behind us? Can we look ahead expectantly and seek greatness instead of assuming it always lies behind us and must be quoted? Can we learn to see and judge things as they are? Can we understand events and others (and ourselves most of all) in a useful, authentic context? Can we learn, perhaps most of all, to act not out of fear or apprehension but out of confidence and clear vision? In one way or another, the dead end of American politics as I write these pieces reminds us that all of these questions now urgently require answers. This is the nature of our moment.

In some ways the American predicament today bears an uncanny resemblance to that of the 1890s. At home we face social, political, and economic difficulties of a magnitude such that they are paralyzing the nation and pulling it apart all at once. Abroad, having fought two costly and pointless wars since 2001, we are challenged to define our place in the world anew—to find a new way of venturing forth into it. The solutions America chose a century ago are not available to us now. But the choices then are starkly ours once again.

Our first choice is to accept the presence of these choices in our national life. This is a decision of considerable importance. To deny it is there comes to a choice in itself—the gravest Americans can make. When America entered history in 2001, it was no one's choice, unless one wants to count Osama bin Laden. This means that America's first choice lies between acceptance and denial. The logic of our national reply seems perfectly evident. To remain as we are, clinging to our myths and all that we once thought made us exceptional, would be to make of our nation an antique, a curiosity of the eighteenth century that somehow survived into the twenty-first. Change occurs in history, and Americans must accept this if they choose to change.

But how does a nation go about accepting fundamental changes in its circumstances—and therefore its identity, its consciousness? How does a nation begin to live in history? In an earlier essay I wrote about what a German thinker has called the culture of defeat and its benefits for the future. Defeat obliges a people to reexamine their understanding of themselves and their place in the world. This is precisely the task lying at America's door, but on the basis of what should Americans take it up? "Defeat" lands hard among Americans. The very suggestion of it is an abrasion. We remain committed to winning the "war on terror" Bush declared in 2001, even if both the term and the notion have come in for scrutiny and criticism. Who has defeated America such that any self-contemplation of the kind I suggest is warranted?

The answer lies clearly before us, for we live among the remains of a defeat of historical magnitude. We need only think carefully to understand it. We need to think of defeat in broader terms—psychological terms, ideological terms, historical terms. We need to think, quite simply, of who we have been—not just to ourselves but to others. Recall our nation's declared destiny before and during its founding. The Spanish-American War and all that followed—in the name of what, these interventions and aggressions? What was it Americans reiterated through all the decades leading to 2001—and, somewhat desperately, beyond that year? It was to remake the world, as Condoleezza Rice so plainly put it. It was to make the world resemble us, such that all of it would have to change and we would not. This dream, this utopia, the prospect of the global society whose imagining made us American, is what perished in 2001. America's fundamentalist idea of itself was defeated on September 11. To put the point another way, America lost its long war against time. This is as real a defeat as any other on a battlefield or at sea. Osama bin Laden and those who gave their lives for his cause spoke for no one but themselves, surely. But they nonetheless gave substantial, dreadful form to a truth that had been a long time coming: The world does not require America to release it into freedom. Often the world does not even mean the same things when it speaks of "freedom," "liberty," and "democracy." And the world is as aware as some Americans are of the dialectic of promise and self-betrayal that runs as a prominent thread through the long fabric of the American past.

Look upon 2001 in this way, and we begin to understand what it was that truly took its toll on the American consciousness. Those alive then had witnessed the end of a long experiment—a hundred years old if one counts from the Spanish war, two hundred to go back to the revolutionary era, nearly four hundred to count from Winthrop and the *Arbella*. I know of no one who spoke of 2001 in these terms at the time: It was unspeakable. But now, after a decade's failed effort to revive the utopian dream and to "create reality," we would do best not only to speak of it but to act with the impossibility of our inherited experiment in mind—confident that there is a truer way of being in the world.

———

Where would an exploration rooted in a culture of defeat land Americans, assuming such an exercise were possible? That it would be a long journey is the first point worth making. There is time no longer for our exceptionalist myths, but to alter our vision of ourselves and ourselves in the world would be no less formidable a task for Americans than it would be (or has been) for anyone else. History suggests that we are counting in decades, for there would be much for Americans to ponder—much that has escaped consideration for many years. History also suggests that the place most logically to begin would be precisely with history itself. It is into history, indeed, that this exploration would deliver us.

In the late 1990s, a time of considerable American triumphalism at home and abroad, the University of Virginia gathered a group of scholars, thinkers, historians, and writers to confer as to an interesting question. The room was filled with liberals and left-liberals. Their question was, "Does America have a democratic mission?"

It seemed significant even that the topic would be framed as a question. Would anyone in Wilson's time have posed one like it? This would not, indeed, have been so just a few years earlier—or a few years later. But it was so then, a line of inquiry launched not quite a decade after the Cold War's end, three years before the events of September 11. Not so curiously, many of those present tended to look to the past. Van Wyck Brooks's noted phrase, "a usable past," was invoked: If we are to understand our future, and whatever our "mission" may be, we had better begin by examining who we have been.

Any such exercise would require a goodly measure of national dedication. It would require "a revolution in spirit," as the social historian Benjamin Barber has put it.[22] But it would bring abundant enhancements. It would begin to transform us. It would make us a larger people in the best sense of the phrase. There is a richness and diversity to the American past that most of us have never registered. Much of it has been buried, it seems to me, because it could not be separated from all that had to be forgotten. Scholarship since the 1960s has unearthed and explored much of this lost history. But scholarship—as has been true for more than a century—proceeds at some distance from public awareness. We now know that the Jeffersonian thread in the American past, for instance, was much more complex, more dense and layered, than Americans have by tradition understood it. In the supposed torpor of the early nineteenth century we find variations of political movements as these were inherited from England. We find among the Democrats the roots of the Populists, the Progressives, democratic socialists, and social democrats. These groups were not infrequently the product of ferment within the liberal wings of various Christian denominations. There was nothing "un-American" about any of them, and all of them were at least partly historicist: They saw America as it was and as it was changing. They understood the need for the nation to move beyond its beginnings to take account of the new.

One need not subscribe to the politics of these or any other formations in history to derive benefit from an enriched and enlivened knowledge of them. They enlarge and revitalize the American notion of "we." And in so doing, history opens up more or less countless alternatives—alternative discourses, alternative ideas of ourselves, alternative politics, alternative institutions. All this is simply to cast history as a source of authentic freedom. At the moment our standard view of the American past lies behind us like a "flattened landscape," as one of our better historians put it some years ago.[23] We are thus unaccustomed to a depth and diversity in our past that present us with a privilege, a benefit, and a duty all at once.

Could Americans bear an unvarnished version of their past—a history with its skin stripped back? History as we now have it seems necessary to bind Americans, to make Americans American. Think merely of the twentieth century and all the wreckage left behind in it in America's name, and it is plain that the question is difficult and without obvious answers. But something salutary is already occurring in our midst. Historians of all kinds have begun new explorations of the past. There are African-American projects, Native American projects, projects concerning foreign affairs, diplomacy, war, and all the secrets these contain. This is the antitradition I mentioned in an earlier essay coming gradually into its own. It is remarkable how sequestered from all this work our public life has proven. The temptations of delusion are always great, and most of America's political figures succumb to them. But time will wear away this hubris. In the best of outcomes, the antitradition will be understood as essential to understanding the tradition.

I once came across a small but very pure example of a nation altering its relation to its past. It was in Guatemala. The long, gruesome civil war there, which ended in the 1990s, had made of the country at once a garden of tragic memories and a nation of forgetters. The Mayans were virtually excluded from history, as they always had been, and the country was deeply divided between *los indigenes* and those of Spanish descent.

Then a journalist named Lionel Toriello, whose forebears had been prominent supporters of the Arbenz government in the 1950s (until Americans arranged a coup in 1954), assembled two million dollars and 156 historians. They spent nearly a decade researching, writing, editing, and peer-reviewing work that was eventually published as a six-volume *Historia General de Guatemala*. Its intent was "pluralistic," Toriello explained during my time with him. It provided as many as three points of view on the periods and events it took up. So it purported to be not a new national narrative so much as an assemblage of narratives from which other narratives could arise. It was a bed of seed, then. Inevitably, Toriello's project had critics of numerous perspectives. Unquestionably, the *Historia General* was the most ambitious history of themselves Guatemalans had ever attempted.[24]

It was an unusual experiment. One of the things Toriello made me realize was that one needs a new vocabulary if one is to explore the past, render it in a new way, and then use it to assume a new direction. A culture of defeat requires that the language must be cleansed. All the presumption buried in it must be identified and removed. Another thing Toriello showed me was that this could be done, even in a small nation torn apart by violence and racial exclusion. The renovated vocabulary arises directly from the history one generates.

None of this, it seems to me, is beyond the grasp of Americans. To consider it so is merely to acknowledge the extent to which the nation famous for its capacity to change cannot change. It is to give in to the temptations of delusion. I do not think "change" took on so totemic a meaning during Barack Obama's 2008 campaign by coincidence. I also think the ridicule of this thought coming from Obama's critics bears interpretation. Change is a testament to strength. But as so often in the past, Americans came to fear what they desired, causing many to take comfort in the next set of constructed political figures promising that, no, nothing at all need change.

An inability to change is symptomatic of a people who consider themselves chosen and who cannot surrender their chosenness. When we look at our nation now, do we see the virtuous republic our history has always placed before us as if it were a sacred chalice? The thought seems preposterous. America was exceptional once, to go straight to the point. But this was not for the reasons Americans thought of themselves as such. America was exceptional during the decades when westward land seemed limitless—from independence until 1890, if we take the census bureau's word for the latter date. For roughly a century, then, Americans were indeed able to reside outside of history—or pretend they did. But this itself, paradoxically, was no more than a circumstance of history. Americans have given the century and some since over to proving what cannot be proved. This is what lends the American century a certain tragic character: It proceeded on the basis of a truth that was merely apparent, not real. Do Americans have a democratic mission? Finally someone has asked. And the only serious answer is, "They never did."

————

Recognizing the truth of this is likely to lead Americans toward a distinction they have heretofore ignored. It is the distinction between a strong nation and one that is merely powerful. One senses that the difference between the two was plain to Americans of the eighteenth century. But then America left this distinction behind. And how fitting, we may now note, that America led the rest of the world into the twentieth century, for if the nineteenth was the century of history, the twentieth was the century of power.

Power is a material capability. It is a possession with no intrinsic vitality of its own. It has to do with method as opposed to purpose or ideals—*techne* as against *telos*. It is sheer means, deployment. Power tends to discourage authentic reflection and considered thought, and, paradoxically, produces a certain weakness in those who have it. This is the weakness that is born of distance from others. In the simplest terms, it is an inability to see and understand others and to tolerate difference. It also induces a crisis of belief. Over time a powerful democracy's faith in itself quivers, while its faith in power and prerogative accumulates. It is true that in the modern world power derives primarily from science. But it is not manipulated—extended or operated, if you like—by scientists. Neither does the use of power require a scientist's intelligence. It is thus that one may find in twentieth-century history modern technologies deployed by people of premodern consciousness. And we cannot exclude Americans when we consider this latter occurrence.

Americans found in power an especially compelling temptation when it began to accrue to them. It was the temptation of certainty without anxiety. It seemed, from the Spanish war onward, within America's grasp to leave behind its old apprehensions at last. The twentieth century thus became the century of power because Americans, as I have already suggested, became ever more reliant upon power alone as its years and decades went by. When power functions by itself, means and ends are inevitably confused; and means, eventually, are taken to be their own end: Power is manifest, that is to say, with no intent other than to manifest itself. The Spanish war was therefore a good introduction to the century we would name for ourselves. Americans claimed to feel deeply for the victims of Spanish oppression, but their own, notably in the Philippines, turned out to be other than an improvement. The true purpose of the Spanish campaign, as the histories make plain, was display—a demonstration of power. At the other end of the century, it is useful to review Washington's various "nation-building" projects in this light.

To reflect upon those final years before 2001, it is not difficult to understand in our contemporary terms the distinction between a powerful nation and a strong one. Strength derives from who one is—it is what one has made of oneself by way of vision, desire, and dedication. It has nothing to do with power as we customarily use this term. Paradoxically, it is a form of power greatly more powerful than the possession of power alone. Strength is a way of being, not a possession. Another paradox: Power renders one vulnerable to defeat or failure, and therefore to fear. Strength renders one not invulnerable—no one ever is—but able to recover from defeats and failures. The history of the past century bears out these distinctions very clearly. Most of all, a strong nation is capable of self-examination and of change. It understands where it is in history—its own and humankind's.

It is curious to return briefly to Woodrow Wilson's list of complaints about American democracy at the start of the American century. "We have not escaped the laws of error that government is heir to," Wilson wrote in 1901. Then came his litany: riots and disorder, an absence of justice, clashes between management and labor, poorly governed cities. "As we grow older, we also grow perplexed and awkward in the doing of justice and in the perfecting and safeguarding of liberty," Wilson concluded. "It is character and good principle, after all, which are to save us, if we are to escape disorder."[25]

Wilson wrote at a curious moment in terms of American power and American strength. What he described, plainly enough, was a nation nervous about losing its strength. And with the invasions of Cuba and the Philippines, America began the effort to make itself a powerful nation instead of a strong one. This was the choice it made when it determined to express itself by way of conquest abroad rather than reformation at home. And from Wilson's day until ours, the progress has proven to be from one to the other, strength to power, as if the one excluded the other. Wilson was a historicist; many intellectuals were by his day. But Wilson was a deeply certain believer, too. He preserved America's exceptionalism as Frederick Jackson Turner did: by placing America ever at history's forward edge.

Among Wilson's useful insights was that Americans possessed a system that did not have the perpetual capacity to self-correct. It required the attention of those living in it. Otherwise it would all come to "disorder." And this is among the things Americans are now faced with in a different way: Theirs is a system, a set of institutions, that yet less possesses the ability to correct its errors and injustices and malfunctions. Time, to put it another way, has taken its toll. This is a stinging judgment, fraught with implications. But at least since the Cold War, it has been necessary to cancel all previous assumptions that American political and social institutions are able to correct themselves as they are currently constituted. The presidential election of 2000 can be considered a tragedy of historic importance in this respect. Institutional frailty is among the attributes of republics as they mature and come to be in need of repair. It is a sign that strength has deserted them. The polity requires tending. Its institutions cannot, any longer, be left to themselves.

―――

Wilson relied much on his thought of character and good principle when he looked forward into the century to come and contemplated America's place in it. Study his writings, and one finds that he counted these among the things that were not supposed to change among Americans. But the war in the Philippines had not ended before there were problems with the character and principles of Americans abroad. American soldiers behaved savagely, by all the historical accounts. Such transgressions would mark American conduct here and there the whole of the American century. Nonetheless, one can count Wilson correct in singling out these characteristics. Character and principle mattered in his time and they matter in ours—even if they might matter by way of their absence.

Wilson thought and wrote and lived out of a tradition that arose during the nation's founding decades. There was little, indeed, that was particularly Wilsonian about Wilsonian idealism. It reflected a certain sensibility, faintly archaic. At the nation's founding Americans took pride in their gentility, sympathy, compassion, and harmoniousness. This was part of their inheritance from the Scottish Enlightenment. They considered themselves a happy people, and their happiness was to be reflected in good works, public virtue, and gracious relations with others. Peacefulness and benevolence were to be expected of any American. These attributes were important. They were how Americans proposed to address the world, and they were some of what set Americans apart: They dreamed of a global society, and it would rest upon a unity of harmonious feeling. Americans, Jefferson said with pride during the republic's early years, were "rational, social, and, if not refined, affectionate."[26] The remark goes to the point precisely.

It is simple enough to see how Wilson fit the mold. But this image of the American man—the "man of feeling," as one eighteenth-century writer depicted him—began to change in the early nineteenth century.[27] There was a devolution in national sentiment. The qualities that had once distinguished the American began to be understood as undesirably aristocratic—even effeminate. We can relate this to the nation's increasing involvement with the westward frontier and the lingering of Old World habits and values among those who remained in the East. The man of feeling gave way to the man of aggressive accomplishment. This was another kind of disposition. Sensibility counted for little when placed against "masculine traits," and "stern virtues," as one scholar has put it: physical strength, of course, but also the ability to subdue others, the desire to assert quickly and decisively, clear-minded judgment, Spartan habits, intellectual simplicity, a hardened sense of honor, sheer manliness in the modern meaning of this term. The man who elevated these qualities as a new emblem of the national character was Andrew Jackson. The instruments of power became important under Jackson. He brought the new American sensibility to the White House when he became president in 1828. By then, Jackson had already disposed of many thousands of "merciless savages" in the Indian wars he fought across the South.

Affect, then, has been a means of patriotic expression since America's founding. But affect is flat and without content—a pose, a reference, a semiotic signal, and no more. Think of Theodore Roosevelt again: He claimed to have overcome his fear by pretending it was not there. It is the quintessential expression of the thought. The place of affect has plainly had consequences by way of America's self-image and what it has done in the world. It is a reflection of American myth in the same way the commonly accepted idea of the American individual is rooted in myth. In this respect, Roosevelt was an almost pure specimen of Jacksonian affect. It was with TR, indeed, that affect—performance and persona, we may say—became part of America's culture of representation. One understands Roosevelt and his desires for himself and his country a great deal better when one considers the man from this perspective. Wilson was a more complex case. He had his ideals, as he is famous for entertaining, but he is somewhat a mystery. He remained pious in the Presbyterian mode when all around him the new imperialism was transforming America into something it was never supposed to be. Next to Roosevelt, he was nearer to a man of eighteenth-century sensibility. But he favored an expansive America himself, apparently impervious to the temptations and dangers. Historians count seven foreign interventions during his time in office. This was the beginning of that constitutional perversion we now call the imperial presidency—apparatus required in the American century.

Later presidents relied to a greater or lesser degree on a Jacksonian affect: Carter not at all; Reagan, an actor just when America needed one, brought almost nothing else to the White House. He gave America a stance and little more. George W. Bush, in turn, brought a badly managed version of Reagan. Bush's two terms, with all the swagger the president rehearsed before the American public, were especially important in this respect. He was the first president to serve after the American century. And his well-known unpopularity abroad still stands as a measure of how inappropriate, how out of phase, the political language spoken by Americans had become once the American century had expired.

To put this point another way, the American century has left Americans with a certain vocabulary or sentiment or posture—I am not sure what to call it—that comes to a mode of addressing the world. The Jacksonian trace is evident. And it is partly with this in mind that I suggest that America is not yet equipped for the twenty-first century. One may assign this thought all manner of meanings. Ours is not a century of globe-engulfing conflict. It is not a century in which power alone will do: In the first ten years of the new era Americans discovered the limits of power palpably enough in their Middle Eastern and West Asian wars. It is not a century of civilizational strife. Nor is it a time when one ideology—anybody's—is destined to prevail, spread benevolently or otherwise around the globe. In all of these ways Americans are ill-prepared—all ready to fight the last war. To take these characteristics of the new century together is to suggest that America faces a kind of national project, for the American sensibility was altered during the American century—distorted at a minimum, possibly damaged—and it is now in need of redress.

Difference and diversity, to take a ready example, will persist in the twenty-first century—they will be celebrated—even as the world becomes one. And in this, history now hands Americans a large irony. They are not accustomed to difference: Historically, they have been attuned to likeness, and likeness has until now meant likeness in the American image. What had been, in the nineteenth century, an intellectual and philosophic distance from Europe became, in the course of the American century, also a political and ideological distance of another magnitude. This distance can be crossed in part if Americans concern themselves with matters of sentiment and posture and distance and proximity, and of character and good principle. This implies the rediscovery of certain parts of the American self that have been obscured.

There is the apparently simple matter of emotion and its place. As I mean it, emotion is a collective aspect of American patriotism. The feelings of Americans, notably a righteous confidence but also fear and anxiety, can be taken as signifiers of loyalty. What difference does it make, then, if Americans consider it important to feel American and mistrust those who do not? It matters much. Emotion of this kind turns out to be the enemy of democracy. This is why, in the eighteenth century, an "enlightened Mind" was posited against "raised Affections." Then as now, feeling reduces politics to sentiment, so making meaning or rational consideration of secondary importance. Feeling is impervious to time and events. It holds one out from history because it is not subject to it in the manner thought is. Thought occurs in response to time's passage and the events occurring in it; thought takes no refuge from history. It is subject to change. Feelings, on the other hand, do not necessarily change regardless of any event or in any time. They bear no relation to chronology. Let us ask ourselves: How well has the privileging of feeling served America over the past century? How well will it serve Americans in the decades to come should they elect to continue feeling first and thinking second?

We come to vigilance—the vigilance Americans have cultivated since the earliest days of the republic. How well does this serve us now? This vigilance, so understandable at the country's start and at other times certainly justified, hardened during the American century, at times taking on aspects of hostility and intolerance and arrogance. In this way, American vigilance came continually to reproduce the need for it. Vigilance, like its close cousin, fear, became normative. It is possible that America's vigilance during the Cold War is unprecedented in history: a vigilance without bottom or end. We still cultivate this vigilance, the enemy now known as "terror." We find our vigilance necessary, exaggerated as it has become, precisely to the extent we have not surrendered the presumptions and practices we considered a providential right during "our" century. There are consequences arising from this. It distances us from others, leaving us unaccustomed to difference. And the hypervigilant society has, once again, a dysfunctional relation to the past. Vigilance fastens people inflexibly to their past (or their past as it is imagined), and they can neither renovate anything nor make anything new. This is vigilance without end. There is no memory—only a fixed past and a consequently fixed present. This, too, is part of the American predicament in the second decade of the twenty-first century.

What are America's first steps forward, then, given these inheritances?

The first is to look and listen in another way, to see and hear from within the space of history. It is to achieve a condition of history with memory. This means to come gradually to accept that one lives in historical time and is as subject to its strictures, its triumphs, and its miseries as anyone else. It means accepting that encounters with others are an essential feature of the world we enter upon. Equally, we must begin to make certain links so that we know who we are and what it is we have been doing—the connections between feeling and time and between vigilance and distance and history are examples. Others have done this, made the passage I am suggesting is upon us. In time, history teaches, it becomes clear that it is more painful to resist this than it is to accept it.

I have become fascinated in the course of writing these essays with the character of early Americans—even if it is an idealized self-image cultivated by slaveowners, murderers of Native Americans, and witch-hunting zealots. A people of sentiment, an affectionate people, a people of virtue and understanding, gentle toward others: It is like holding up a mirror and not recognizing the face staring back from it. Even the vocabulary: It has a faintly eighteenth-century scent to it. Mercy Otis Warren's *History* is full of this terminology. But consider these attributes as they might be understood in our time. There are twenty-first-century ways to describe them—terms developed among philosophers concerned with the progress of human ties. We can now speak of empathy, meaning that one sees another not simply as an object but as another subject—an equivalent. This is achieved through a recognition of another's perspective, intentions, and emotions. This makes one's objective experiences available to all other subjects: One feels oneself to be a subject among other subjects. These concepts are drawn from what I will call for simplicity's sake the discourse of self and Other, which developed in Europe at mid-twentieth century. This line of thought did not travel well in America. Like the ideas that animated Europe in the nineteenth century, it arrived among Americans in brackets: This is what they are up to across the water. The discourse of self and Other concerns the evolution of human relations, which are recognized as plural as opposed to unified. And human relations, as the philosopher Emmanuel Lévinas pointed out, take place in time. As I have already suggested, time is our shared medium.[28]

In all of these matters Americans grew deficient during the last century. One must have a strong sense of self to encounter others and accept difference, and Americans came to lack this. The Cold War, in particular, produced a certain personality such that the concepts I have just described may seem foreign, or fey, or faintly beside the point. This reflects our error. And to understand this error now would equip Americans with the vocabulary, the character and good principle that will be useful in the century to come. To know others well, or let us say better than Americans do, will be part of what it means to be a strong nation in the twenty-first century. The thought seems to imply a reconstruction of the American identity. This is precisely the intended meaning. The project has been accomplished before.

Two American figures are worth considering in this context. I have already noted both. One is Wendell Willkie, the failed Republican presidential candidate in 1940. Midway through World War II Roosevelt dispatched Willkie to tour the world and describe his thoughts as to how our planet was likely to emerge from the war. *One World* was the result, a now-forgotten book that was at the time widely and eagerly read.[29] The other figure is Jimmy Carter, our thirty-ninth president. Both of these men are often sources of derision among Americans. A certain wide-eyed fatuousness commonly attaches to them. I am not unaware of their reputations in this regard. I simply take issue with such presuppositions. In my view both represented lost opportunities: Willkie by way of the idealism of the immediate postwar period, which was palpable even if brief, and Carter in the chance to begin again in a new direction during the post-Vietnam period—also a window briefly opened. Both men displayed many of the qualities the current century will ask of us. Both were clear in the matter of history. Both drew from rich but obscured traditions in the American past. Both understood, it seems to me, the difference between strength and power. Both knew that the former requires more courage than the latter—the courage to interact with those of different beliefs, the confidence to stay the use of force, the poise to put America's inbred fear aside and act not out of vengeance but from considered wisdom.

We should remember figures such as Willkie and Carter better than we do. It would enlarge our idea of who we are and of what it means to be American. The inability to advance beyond common caricatures of these two and others is nothing more than a measure of our inability to reimagine ourselves. It is by way of such people, whoever they turn out to be, that we can regain some realistic idea of utopia—utopia in this sense meaning simply a future that transcends the present. Democracy has always been fragile—as delicate as a length of eighteenth-century lace. It is evanescent: Much is done in its name that is not genuinely a reflection of it. Our moment in history, our debt to the future, requires us to begin conceiving of an extensively reorganized society. It requires demilitarization and re-democratization, to take ready examples.

Our difficulties in both respects reflect a failure to keep pace with the progress we have engendered, with the speed we have ourselves created—with history's acceleration, which is, in the end, our own doing. "The acquisition of new implements of power too swiftly outruns the necessary adjustment of habits and ideas to the novel conditions created by their use." That is the historian Carl Becker, lecturing at Stanford in 1935.[30] It is prescient by half a century, perhaps more. The core issue is one of control—control over what we are able to do. Closer to our time, the French thinker Paul Virilio suggests that we have to add to our technological revolutions a revolution of consciousness, of ideas, such that our thinking and our purposes are elevated to a value equivalent to our capabilities. We do not typically recognize it, but at present these are unmatched. Science can no longer converge with technology alone, Virilio argues; in our time it must also be animated by philosophy.[31] This is one of the twentieth century's more profound failings.

All this begins to define our responsibility as we free ourselves of national myths. If there is a case for optimism, it lies in a reconstitution of our thought, our intelligence, in this fashion. Much that is now accepted as fated and beyond our capacity to change must be understood otherwise. We live within a strange contradiction, sour fruit of the century now gone by. In the spheres of science and technology we assume ourselves to be without limit. But we give ourselves no credit for being able to make social, economic, or political change—anthropological change altogether. In 2012 our shared supposition is that there are no new ideas—only old ideas to be tried again. That is what is enacted in our culture of representation today. And we must advance beyond it.

There are implications. Such an endeavor will unmask us. We would have to regain a lost confidence among us in "we." We would have to look forward and see that a new kind of society is possible. And the project requires us—and notably our leaders—to begin speaking in a language of authentic alternatives.

———

The claim to exceptionalism is remarkable for its resilience. Little else remains of the old, not-much-regarded myths. But even now America as the world's exception is asserted at home and abroad. It is a consequence of history, perhaps: America was an idea before it was a nation. "In 2008, it is absolutely clear that we will be involved in nation-building for years to come," Condoleezza Rice, Bush's secretary of state, wrote that year in *Foreign Affairs*.[32] It was Bush's last in office. Woodrow Wilson could have asserted this same remark a hundred years earlier. It is pre-historicist. It is exceptionalism as baldly stated as it can be in policy terms—in terms of what America proposes to do. No lessons drawn from the previous century? One would think America remains deaf and blind even now.

Nations are eventually made by those who live in them, no matter whether it is in a great power's interest to fashion one or another of them to its liking. Americans should know this better than anyone, though the point seems to elude them. Now they have an opportunity to learn this truth from the Afghanistan and Iraq wars. Both have been failures in the standard sense of an American "mission," or as new demonstrations of American prerogative. In both nations, what will finally well up from the Afghan and Iraqi earth will be by way of millions of conversations, interests, persuasions, alliances, oppositions—the very fiber of a political culture, none of it having anything to do with America. As for Americans, they were warriors in wars they did not understand. I do not think this will any longer be possible in the century we inhabit. And in the best of outcomes, those final two failures will lead to what I will call a post-Wilsonian idealism. It may be that there is nothing to salvage from Wilson's thought, for we have found it defective from the first. But for the sake of continuity let us assume it is something to build upon.

The turning forward of the Wilsonian ethos would involve restraint as much as it would assertion. It would also mean accepting that what America exported in the way of "democracy" during the twentieth century was often fraudulent, a duping, a false promise. It would mean looking back at America's democracy and recognizing that Americans alone had to make it. Is this to say that post-Wilsonian Americans are to sit and watch as others suffer? My answers to this are two. First of all, there is little doubt that the span of American interventions beginning in 1898 and ending now in Afghanistan has caused more suffering than it has relieved. This is so by a wide margin, to put the point mildly. Second, the post-Wilsonian would act abroad rigorously according to his or her ideals and not some hollowed-out version of them, as even Wilson did. He or she would also act with the greatest of delicacy. Understanding one's own history also means being attentive to others'. The post-Wilsonian will be supremely mindful of this, elevating self-determination to the highest of values.

We have distinguished between relative and absolute decline, noting that the former is inevitable in an age of rising powers. Many of us believe ours to be the "Pacific century," implying that America's frontage on the Pacific lake will be its salvation. I do not think this will prove so: The same was said at the end of the nineteenth century. America is a Pacific power; it is now called upon to recognize that this does not make it an Asian power. By the same token, it does not seem to me that we have entered an "Asian century," either. It will be a century that cannot be named, in my view, because too great a variety of people will contribute to it.

This is a positive prospect. But much hangs on whether Americans are capable of accepting it as such. For at the horizon, relative and absolute decline turn out to meet. If Americans do not accept the advance of history, relative decline will devolve into absolute decline: The rise of others will translate into America being left uncompetitively behind because it has not understood the tasks at hand. But if Americans are able to accept a place in the world that is distinct from all they have assumed since 1898, the nation's relative decline will prove an experience of benefit. It will change the American character, so far as one can speak of such a thing, and much for the better. It will alter Americans' stance toward others and their stances toward one another. It will engender that process of self-examination I have already dwelled upon, leading Americans to recognize the tasks before them. Here is the paradox of our moment: Only if Americans resist the defeat I have described will they be defeated. In our refusal to admit defeat would lie our true defeat, for we would have no access to renewal, we would not be able to think anew.

I propose in these pieces the taking of an immense risk. It is the risk of living without things that are linked in the American psyche: the protection of our exceptionalism, the armor of our triumphalist nationalism, our fantastical idea of the individual and his or her subjectivity. For Americans to surrender this universe of belief, emotion, and thought may seem the utmost folly. A century ago Americans flinched at the prospect. What followed was often called heroic, but in many cases it was just the opposite, for the American century was so often an exercise in avoidance of genuinely defined responsibility. True enough, it ended as it began, with uncertainty and choices. But the outcome need not be the same now, for there is too much more to be gained than lost this time.

———

"The transformation of the old sense of a glorious national destiny into the sense of a serious national purpose will inevitably tend to make the popular realization of the Promise of American Life both more explicit and more serious."[33]

One must marvel at the clarity with which Herbert Croly was able to see his time for what it was. And consider with wonder, too, the extent to which Croly's best-known book, *The Promise of American Life*, remains a guide to the tasks Americans now find before them. Croly understood change to be essentially creative; history was infinitely creative. And to know these things is to be truly modern in the best sense of this term.

He was wrong about certain things. He did not surrender his own idea of American exceptionalism: He held it, indeed, rather high. He critiqued with considerable vigor "the prevalent mixture of optimism, fatalism, and conservatism" he found among Americans. But he parsed his criticism carefully, for he shared the orthodox view that the meaning of America lay always in front of it. "The fault in the vision of our national future possessed by the ordinary American does not consist in the expectation of some continuity of achievement," Croly wrote. "It consists rather in the expectation that the familiar benefits will continue to accumulate automatically."[34]

This passage goes to the heart of Croly's achievement—or one of them, at any rate. He understood our proper relation to the American past; more energetically did he recognize that Americans could not be bound by it. His attitude toward tradition presages those I have noted in an earlier essay: One honors tradition by adding to it, not by making it a chain binding people such that they cannot act. "That tradition may be transformed," Croly wrote of America's, "but it will not be violated."[35]

It is Croly's argument for the need for action and transformation that has drawn me frequently to a book now more than a century old. It is by way of these that a people can advance from a belief in destiny to a commitment to purpose. The distinction, of course, is key. Destiny brings with it no authentic sense of responsibility. Indeed, it leaves a people in a state of irresponsibility. In the extreme it infantilizes a society—it is not too strong a term—for there are few duties other than each to himself or herself. The life of a nation will seem to advance as a matter of history's gift. Destiny leaves people free to pursue, as Croly put it, "the abundant satisfactions of individual desires," for nothing else need be done—not to the ever-wise market, not in one's infallible political and social institutions. "The fulfillment of the American Promise was considered inevitable," Croly wrote, "because it was based upon a combination of self-interest and the natural goodness of human nature."[36] This is an eighteenth-century conception of both self-interest and nature. We cannot, Croly was telling his contemporaries, any longer live this way.

But what are a people to do when these happy conditions—notably the virtue of individual self-interest—prove to have been betrayals? It is Croly's word, and his answer was to leave behind destiny and all the myths supporting it and embrace a national purpose. I can think of no more salutary a project for Americans to undertake today. Purpose requires that a society respond to its conditions. In this way it requires responsibility. The future that was once a given must now be "planned and constructed rather than fulfilled of its own momentum," as Croly put it. In the American case this is especially sensitive with regard to markets, since the neoliberal belief in the perfection of markets remains intact in the face of a great deal of evidence to the contrary.

Purpose is also a national matter, so the nation must articulate its purpose to itself. It requires self-discipline and a new relation between the individual and society: "a large measure of individual subordination and self-denial," in Croly's words. Croly was a Progressive and held to Progressive beliefs. "In becoming responsible for the subordination of the individual to the demand of a dominant and constructive national purpose," he wrote, "the American state will in effect be making itself responsible for a morally and socially desirable distribution of wealth."[37] This was, in Croly's day, acceptable public comment. It had echoes in the eighteenth and nineteenth centuries—many of them—and it still counted among what was sayable, for there had been no Russian Revolution, no Cold War, and no elevation of neoliberal economic thought to the plane of holiness. It was Croly's way of addressing the root of the social problem, which was his primary concern. It was his way of suggesting that responsibility was inevitably bound up with history. To declare a purpose, to accept responsibility for it: This was to understand one's place in the human story. It was not only to accept the occurrence of change but also actively to pursue it.

———

All of what Croly wrote seems today to be predicated on the thought that a people can achieve an objective view of themselves and then act according to it. This is a desirable prospect; possibly it is implicit in my description of the self-examination a nation undergoes in the wake of a defeat. But is this kind of objectivity possible? In the American case, objectivity would involve putting down all our national myths and stories as if they were so much clanking armor after the battle is done.

"Nobody knows what it would be like to try to be objective when attempting to decide what one's country really is, what its history really means, any more than when answering the question of who one really is oneself, what one's individual past adds up to." This is Richard Rorty, the noted political philosopher, lecturing at Harvard in 1997. We may know little or nothing of what it means to be objective, for objectivity is an ideal ever to be striven for but never (by definition) to be reached. Many of us know this striving, however—the "trying to be" Rorty discounts. "We raise questions about our individual or national identity," Rorty quickly adds, "as part of the process of deciding what we will do next, what we will try to become."[38]

This is precisely where America stood in the late 1990s, when Rorty lectured, and precisely where it is today. It is in this sense (among numerous others) that the intervening years encompass so much that must be counted wasteful. The armor of our national mythology is no longer of use. Destiny has deserted us. Americans must determine anew their individual and national identities—the one closely bound to the other. How can one manage this—how an entire nation? Objectively? We have but the ideal.

Again, I do not see that this is an insurmountable challenge. Nations define themselves by way of ideals but also by way of actions taken. The one reflects the other. The years of the Bush presidency defined America as radically individual, if not isolated, defiant of global opinion, belittling of cooperation, vastly overdependent on power, and short on imaginative ideas. This has already begun to change. We appear to have learned much from Bush's wars. I question whether America is capable of electing another George W.

Bush, even as it continues, five years after he left office, trying to repair the damage he wrought.

Action and purpose: They are bound as one. What one does, how one exerts oneself upon the world—these define one's purpose. And it is not as if the twenty-first century has left us with little to do, as many Americans seem to have understood during the autumn of 2001. Purpose, as that singular season illustrated, arises from a clear view of historical circumstances. In America's case, destiny defined a century of interventions and "missions" supposedly based on democratic ideals. With purpose, we can proceed toward the construction of a global community of nations—an obvious task for us all. And in the course of this undertaking, a turn toward post-Wilsonian idealism as I have described this would almost certainly win worldwide applause.

We are left with the question of self-understanding. And for this we can return briefly but usefully to Herbert Croly. "The very genuine experience upon which American optimistic fatalism rests," he wrote, "is equivalent, because of its limitations, to a dangerous inexperience, and of late years an increasing number of Americans have been drawing this inference. They have been coming to see themselves more as others see them."[39] Croly was overoptimistic, or premature by a century, or both. But there is no better salve for the lesioned national psyche than to assume a perspective on oneself from another's point of view. Who are we? Who do others think we are? The questions are not unrelated, the one informing the other.

——

To take up the questions I have engaged is to open oneself to dangers. Is it possible for an American to write from outside the tradition that is critiqued or, despite all efforts, do we all fall within it? Is all critique canceled in "the carnival of the image" we have made of so much of our public life?[40] Does the work come to some kind of punishing jeremiad—the latest in a long line? Is it secretly optimistic, with all its "we's" and "ours"? Is there some errant exceptionalism to be detected in these pages? All we need do is recognize our many tasks and we shall accomplish them as we always have: Is this the hidden presumption?

None of these propositions describes my purpose, for they are together part of the same dialectic—one that Americans would do well to advance beyond. A renovated identity and a nationalism that can stand without the support of myth are high among my concerns. So is a society that can live without its inbred fear of others, its tendency to paranoia, and its habit of representation. The imperative now is to look forward, building outward from the tradition. But even if we come to recognize the need of these things, there is no guarantee we will find it possible to get them done. There is no certainty we will construct or reconstruct a "we." There is no guarantee we will find the language the projects before us require. That language is not in this book; it would be quite different from what I have written. In short, our passage from myth to history brings many chances with it, but they are chances worth taking for the sake of a future that hangs in the balance.

I have ranged rather widely in these pieces, I am aware. There is a purpose to this. Our nationalism, our individualist identities and subjectivity, our "national character," our taste for imperial power: Much has been written about each of these. But it seemed to me vital to reach a point of reckoning such that these could be treated together. I do not believe that any of these aspects of American life, conduct, and sensibility is separable from any other. Each is an expression of the others. They all represent aspects of a kind of psychological investment. We must understand this investment—a heavy investment indeed—if we are to make authentic sense of such terms as "we" or "Americans," carelessly used expressions within which lie layers of complexity we would do well to unearth. Just as our extreme idea of the individual cannot be separated from how America acted in the twentieth century, the new century requires a new idea of ourselves. To put the point another way, Americans will need a fundamentally new means of venturing forth in the world if they are to succeed in a fundamentally new time.

I have written primarily to describe the unfinished work—and the choices, too—lying before Americans as they leave an era behind and enter a new one. Implicit in these essays is the thought that much of what was taken to be heroism during the American century had at least an element of cowardice in it. It is a strong word. But too often Americans flinched from genuine responsibilities—at home and abroad, to themselves and to others—and escaped into adventures that power alone made possible. Myth was always the cover for these escapes, invoked by way of representation—symbol, image, and allusion. Now we find that both myth and representation serve only to keep our gaze fixed behind us; they retard us in this way. Are we to flinch again now, at the merest suggestion that there is work ahead of us to do? History and myth: They are the protagonist and antagonist of these essays. Choosing between the two—the one requiring courage, the other giving shabby shelter—is the most important decision Americans face. From it, most others will follow.

It is in this context that I am especially aroused by the notion of decline. Five years before I began these essays, one was counted a pariah for raising even the question of it. Now Americans cannot stop thinking and talking about it, as if it is inevitable. I do not know which is worse. There is much history in both cases: the old "optimistic fatalism" Croly wrote of, and then the inbred fear of internal decay that dates to the seventeenth century. Few of us seem to understand the matter as one of choice—choice and responsibility. "Is America over?" *Foreign Affairs* wondered on the cover of one of its recent editions.[41] It is precisely the kind of language America needs to leave behind. The answer, in any event, is no—only the mythological rendition.

NOTES

Introduction

1. Friedrich Nietzsche, "On the Uses and Disadvantages of History for Life," in *Untimely Meditations* (Cambridge: Cambridge University Press, 1997), 61.

2. C. Vann Woodward, "The Irony of Southern History," in *The Burden of Southern History*, 3rd ed. (Baton Rouge: Louisiana State University Press, 1993), 193.

3. E. R. A. Seligman, "Economics and Social Progress," *Papers of the American Economics Association*, 3rd series, 4 (1903):59.

History Without Memory

1. Henry Nash Smith, *Virgin Land: The American West as Symbol and Myth* (Cambridge: Harvard University Press, 1950), vii.

2. John Winthrop, "A Model of Christian Charity," reproduced in *The Puritans in America: A Narrative Anthology,* ed. Alan Heimart and Andrew Delbanco (Cambridge: Harvard University Press, 1985), 91.

3. Cotton Mather, *Nehemias Americanus: The Life of John Winthrop, Esq., Governor of the Massachusetts Colony* (London, 1702), reproduced in Sacran

Bercovich, *The Puritan Origins of the American Self* (1975; New Haven: Yale University Press, 2011), 189.

4. See Norman Cohn, *The Pursuit of the Millennium: Revolutionary Millenarians and Mystical Anarchists of the Middle Ages,* rev. ed. (New York: Oxford University Press, 1970).

5. Lewis Mumford, *Sticks and Stones: A Study of American Architecture and Civilization* (New York: Boni and Liveright, 1924), 14.

6. James Rosier, *George Waymouth: The Wonderful River, 1605,* reproduced in *The New Land,* ed. Philip Viereck (New York: John Day, 1967), 65–74.

7. Pierre Biard, *Father Biard: A Man of God Among Savaged Europeans and Natives, 1611,* reproduced in Viereck, *New Land,* 139–49.

8. Michael Wigglesworth, quoted in "God's Controversy with New England," *Proceedings of the Massachusetts Historical Society* 12 (1871–73): 83–84, and reproduced in Smith, *Virgin Land,* 4.

9. Sacran Bercovich, *The American Jeremiad* (Madison: University of Wisconsin Press, 1978); see especially "The Typology of America's Mission," 93–131.

10. See Carl Becker, *The Heavenly City of the Eighteenth-Century Philosophers* (New Haven: Yale University Press, 1932), and Stow Persons, "The Cyclical Theory of History in Eighteenth Century America," *American Quarterly* 6 (1954): 147–63.

11. Mircea Eliade, *The Myth of the Eternal Return; Or, Cosmos and History,* trans. *Willard R. Trask,* Bollingen Series 46 (Princeton: Princeton University Press, 1991). This volume also provides a fulsome examination of *illud tempus,* Eliade's "sacred time." In addition to readings in Eliade, I have also drawn upon Henri-Charles Puech, "Gnosis and Time," in *Man and Time: Papers from the Eranos Yearbooks, trans. Ralph Manheim,* Bollingen Series 30, no. 3 (New York: Pantheon, 1957), 38–84.

12. See Catherine L. Albanese, *Sons of the Fathers: The Civil Religion of the American Revolution* (Philadelphia: Temple University Press, 1976).

13. The most prominent scholars to develop the millenarian interpretation of America's founding are Perry Miller, *Errand into the Wilderness* (Cambridge: Harvard University Press, 1956), and *Nature's Nation* (Cambridge: Harvard University Press, 1967); Bercovich, *Puritan Origins* and *American Jeremiad;* and Ernest Tuveson, *Redeemer Nation: The Idea of America's Millennial Role* (Chicago: University of Chicago Press, 1968). I have also drawn from James West Davidson, *The Logic of Millennial Thought: Eighteenth-Century New England* (New Haven: Yale University Press, 1977).

14. See Davidson, *Logic of Millennial Thought,* 12.

15. See Henry Tudor, *Political Myth* (New York: Praeger, 1972).

16. See G. K. Chesterton, "What I Saw in America," *The Collected Works of G. K. Chesterton* (San Francisco: Ignatius, 1990), 21: 41–45.

17. See Izrahiah Wetmore, *Sermon Preached Before the General Assembly* (New London, Conn., 1773), 5–6, 19; Henry Cummings, *A Sermon, Preached at Billerica, on the 23rd of November 1775* (Worcester, Mass., 1776), 6, 9. Both passages are cited in Davidson, *Logic of Millennial Thought*, 233–34.

18. Mercy Otis Warren, *History of the Rise, Progress, and Termination of the American Revolution*, 3 vols. (Boston: E. Larkin, 1805), 1: 225. The work is reproduced in a facsimile edition by AMS Press, New York, 1970.

19. Philip Payson, Election Sermon, May 27, 1778, in *The Pulpit of the American Revolution*, ed. John Wingate Thornton (New York: Burt Franklin, 1970), 353. See also chapter 1 of Albanese, *Sons of the Fathers*.

20. See Maya Jasanoff, *Liberty's Exiles: American Loyalists in the Revolutionary World* (New York: Knopf, 2011). See also Philip Davidson, *Propaganda and the American Revolution: 1763–1783* (Chapel Hill: University of North Carolina Press, 1941).

21. J. G. A. Pocock, *The Machiavellian Moment: Florentine Political Thought and the Atlantic Republican Tradition* (Princeton: Princeton University Press, 1975). See also Dorothy Ross, "The Liberal Tradition Revisited and the Republican Tradition Addressed," in *New Directions in American Intellectual History*, ed. John Higham and Paul Keith Conklin (Baltimore: Johns Hopkins University Press, 1979), 116–31.

22. From *Notes on Virginia*, cited in "Thomas Jefferson: A Portrait," in Claude G. Bowers, *Jefferson and Hamilton: The Struggle for Democracy in America* (Boston: Houghton Mifflin, 1925), 105.

23. Kissinger addressed the Boston World Affairs Council. See *Time*, March 22, 1976, 6. Bush addressed a joint session of Congress on September 20, 2001. Romney addressed the Virginia Military Institute on October 8, 2012; *New York Times*, October 9, 2012.

24. Hofstadter is quoted often on this point. My reference is to Seymour Martin Lipset, *American Exceptionalism: A Double-Edged Sword* (New York: Norton, 1996): "It has been our fate as a nation not to have ideologies, but to be one" (18).

25. Lipset, *American Exceptionalism*, 17.

26. Warren, *History of the Rise*, 3: 435–36.

27. John A. Schutz and Douglas Adair, eds. *The Spur of Fame: Dialogues of John Adams and Benjamin Rush, 1805–1813* (San Marino, Calif.: Huntington

Library, 1966), 185–87. See also Michael Kammen, *Mystic Chords of Memory: The Transformation of Tradition in American Culture* (New York: Vintage, 1993).

28. Warren used the phrase (and referred to the thought) frequently. See especially *History of the Rise,* 3: 434–35.

29. G. W. F. Hegel, *The Philosophy of History,* trans. J. Sibree (New York: Willey, 1944), 86–87. See also Christopher Coker, *The Twilight of the West* (Boulder, Colo.: Westview, 1998), 6–8.

30. See David Lowenthal, *The Past Is a Foreign Country* (Cambridge: Cambridge University Press, 1985), 110.

31. D. H. Lawrence, "John Galsworthy," in *Selected Essays* (Harmondsworth: Penguin, 1950), 222.

32. Walter Gropius, "Tradition and the Center," *Harvard Alumni Bulletin* 53, no. 2 (1950): 69.

A Culture of Representation

1. Quoted in Edmund Morris, *The Rise of Theodore Roosevelt* (New York: Random House, 1979), 674. See also Ivan Musicant, *Empire by Default: The Spanish-American War and the Dawn of the American Century* (New York: Henry Holt, 1998), 383–84.

2. Musicant, *Empire by Default,* 386.

3. Morris, *Rise of Theodore Roosevelt,* 33. See also John Milton Cooper, Jr., *The Warrior and the Priest: Woodrow Wilson and Theodore Roosevelt* (Cambridge: Belknap Press of Harvard University Press, 1983), 8, and Theodore Roosevelt, *The Works of Theodore Roosevelt,* vol. 20, *An Autobiography* (New York: Scribner, 1926), 55.

4. Cooper, *Warrior and the Priest,* 8.

5. Quoted in David Traxel, *1898: The Birth of the American Century* (New York: Knopf, 1998), 179.

6. Ibid., 116.

7. Wayne H. Morgan, *William McKinley and His America* (Syracuse: Syracuse University Press, 1963), 372.

8. Traxel, *1898,* 125.

9. Roosevelt, *Works,* vol. 11, *The Rough Riders,* 63.

10. Stephen Crane, *Wounds in the Rain: War Stories* (New York: Frederick A. Stokes, 1900). See also Traxel, *1898,* 173.

11. In this section I have drawn upon Henry Tudor, *Political Myth* (New York: Praeger, 1972), and Jürgen Habermas, *The Structural Transformation of*

the Public Sphere: An Inquiry into a Category of Bourgeois Society, trans. Thomas Burger (Cambridge: MIT Press, 1993).

12. A. N. Whitehead, *Symbolism: Its Meaning and Effect,* Barbour-Page Lectures, University of Virginia, 1927 (New York: Capricorn, 1959), 6–7.

13. Traxel, *1898,* 147–48.

14. Auguste Comte, *The Positivist Philosophy of Auguste Comte,* 3 vols., trans. Harriet Martineau (London: George Bell, 1896), 1: 15. See also Gillis J. Harp, *Positivist Republic: Auguste Comte and the Reconstruction of American Liberalism, 1865–1920* (University Park: Pennsylvania State University Press, 1995), 11–12.

15. Ernest Renan, *History of the People of Israel: From the Time of Hezekiah Till the Return from Babylon,* vol. 3 (Boston: Roberts Brothers, 1894), 203.

16. William P. Trent et al., eds., "Later Philosophy," *Cambridge History of American Literature,* vol. 3 (Cambridge: Cambridge University Press, 1943), 229–30. See also Harp, *Positivist Republic,* 5. Throughout the present passage I am also indebted to Dorothy Ross, *The Origins of American Social Science* (Cambridge: Cambridge University Press, 1991).

17. Henry Adams, *The Education of Henry Adams: An Autobiography* (Boston: Houghton Mifflin, 1918), 239.

18. David Levin, *History as a Romantic Art* (Stanford: Stanford University Press, 1959); see especially 3–23. See also J. Franklin Jameson, *The History of Historical Writing in America* (Boston: Houghton Mifflin, 1891), and Dorothy Ross, "Historical Consciousness in Nineteenth Century America," *American Historical Review* 89 (1984): 909–28.

19. Quoted in Levin, *History as a Romantic Art,* 3.

20. The quoted passages from Bancroft are drawn from Frank Friedel, ed., *The Golden Age of American History* (New York: George Braziller, 1959).

21. The Rev. Edward Brooks, quoted in Lawrence B. Davis, *Immigrants, Baptists, and the Protestant Mind in America* (Urbana: University of Illinois Press, 1973), 64.

22. Josiah Strong, *Our Country: Its Possible Future and Its Present Crisis* (New York: Baker and Taylor, 1885), 2.

23. Ibid., viii.

24. Frederick Jackson Turner, "The Significance of the Frontier in American History," in *Rereading Frederick Jackson Turner: "The Significance of the Frontier in American History" and Other Essays* (New York: Henry Holt, 1994), 31–60 for all citations.

25. The historian Frederick L. Paxson is especially interesting on this point. See *When the West Is Gone,* Colver Lectures, Brown University, 1929 (New York: Henry Holt, 1930).

26. Woodrow Wilson, "Democracy and Efficiency," *Atlantic Monthly,* March 1901, 289–99 for all citations.

27. See, for instance, William Appleman Williams, *The Tragedy of American Diplomacy* (Cleveland: World, 1959), chapter 2, "The Imperialism of Idealism," 45–60.

28. Gertrude Stein, *The Autobiography of Alice B. Toklas,* A Project Gutenberg Australia ebook, no. 0608711.txt, posted 2006, www.gutenberg.net.au/ebooks06/0608711.txt, chapter 4, "Gertrude Stein Before She Came to Paris," accessed August 24, 2012.

29. Wilson, "Democracy and Efficiency," 297.

Cold War Man

1. Geoffrey C. Ward, *Lindbergh,* Insignia Films for *The American Experience* (Boston: WGBH, 1990), http://www.pbs.org/wgbh/amex/lindbergh/filmmore/transcript/transcript1.html, transcript accessed October 4, 2001.

2. The Morand quotations are from *De la vitesse* (Paris: Vingtième Siècle, Éditions Kra, 1929). The translations are mine. See also Paul Virilio, *Speed and Politics: An Essay in Dromology,* trans. Mark Polizotti (New York: Foreign Agents Series, Semiotext(e), 1986).

3. John Dewey, *The Quest for Certainty: A Study of the Relation of Knowledge and Action* (New York: Minton, Balch, 1929), 3.

4. Ibid., 9.

5. See Robert D. Ward. "The Origin and Activities of the National Security League, 1914–1919," *Mississippi Valley Historical Review* 47, no. 1 (1960): 51–65.

6. Lawrence S. Wittner, *American Intervention in Greece, 1943–1949* (New York: Columbia University Press, 1982), 71. See also Dean Acheson, *Present at the Creation: My Years at the State Department* (New York: Norton, 1969), chapter 25, "The Truman Doctrine," 220–35.

7. Louis J. Halle, *The Cold War as History* (New York: Harper and Row, 1967), 120–21. See also Wittner, *American Intervention in Greece,* 78.

8. Acheson, *Present at the Creation,* 222. See also Wittner, *American Intervention in Greece,* 80, where the reproduction of the speech is slightly at variance.

9. Henry Adams to Brooks Adams, August 10, 1902, in *Letters of Henry Adams,* ed. Worthington Chauncy Ford (Boston: Houghton Mifflin, 1938), 2: 391–92. See also Henry Steele Commager, *The American Mind: An Interpretation of American Thought and Character Since the 1880s* (New York: Bantam, 1970), 293.

10. Rexford G. Tugwell, "Experimental Economics," in *The Trend in Economics* (New York: Knopf, 1924), 421. See also Dorothy Ross, *The Origins of American Social Science* (Cambridge: Cambridge University Press, 1991), chapter 10, "Scientism," 390–470.

11. Philip Mirowsky, *Machine Dreams: Economics Becomes a Cyborg Science* (Cambridge: Cambridge University Press, 2002), 162–69.

12. Vannevar Bush, *Science—The Endless Frontier: A Report to the President on a Program for Postwar Scientific Research* (Washington, D.C.: National Science Foundation, [1945]).

13. Ibid., 6.

14. Ibid., 2.

15. Ibid., 11.

16. See James Ledbetter, *Unwarranted Influence: Dwight D. Eisenhower and the Military-Industrial Complex* (New Haven: Yale University Press, 2011).

17. Executive Order: National Defense Resources Preparedness, March 16, 2012, http://www.whitehouse.gov/the-press-office/2012/03/16/executive-order-national-defense-resources-preparedness, accessed August 24, 2012. I am grateful to Professor Herb Bix, late of Binghamton University, for drawing my attention to this and other executive orders enacted during the Bush and Obama administrations.

18. Paul Hazard, *European Thought in the Eighteenth Century,* trans. J. Lewis May (New Haven: Yale University Press, 1954); see especially chapter 2, "Happiness," 14–25. See also Pascal Bruckner, *L'Euphorieperpétuelle: Essaisur le devoir de bonheur* (Paris: Grasset et Fasquelle, 2000).

19. C. Wright Mills, *The Power Elite* (Oxford: Oxford University Press, 1956), 274.

20. Hannah Arendt, *The Human Condition* (Chicago: University of Chicago Press, 1958), 231.

21. Jean-Pierre Dupuy, *On the Origins of Cognitive Science: The Mechanization of the Mind* (Cambridge: MIT Press, 2009). See especially "The Self-Mechanized Mind," 3–26.

22. See Laura McEnaney, *Civil Defense Begins at Home: Militarization Meets Everyday Life in the Fifties* (Princeton: Princeton University Press, 2000).

23. See Philip Mirowski, "Realism and Neoliberalism: From Reactionary Modernism to Postwar Conservatism," in *The Invention of International Relations Theory: Realism, the Rockefeller Foundation, and the 1954 Conference on Theory*, ed. Nicholas Guilhot (New York: Columbia University Press, 2011), 210–38.

24. Henry Steele Commager, *The Defeat of America: Presidential Power and the American Character* (New York: Simon and Schuster, 1968). See especially 9–47.

25. Ibid., 32.

26. Cited in Frank Ninkovich, *The Wilsonian Century: U.S. Foreign Policy Since 1900* (Chicago: University of Chicago Press, 1999), 234.

27. The Carter quotations are cited ibid., 248–49.

28. Wolfgang Schivelbusch, *The Culture of Defeat: On National Trauma, Mourning, and Recovery,* trans. Jefferson Chase (New York: Metropolitan, Picador edition), 2004. My debt to Mr. Schivelbusch's thinking, as I have applied it to present purposes, will be evident.

29. Reinhart Koselleck, "Erfahrungswandel und Methodenwechsel: Eine historisch-anthropologissche Skizze," in *Historiche Methode,* ed. Christian Meier and Jorn Rosen (Munich, 1988), cited in Schivelbusch, *Culture of Defeat,* 4.

30. Charles Augustin Sainte-Beuve, *Les Cahiers de Sainte-Beuve* (Paris: Alphonse Lemerre, 1876). For the translation I have relied upon Geoffrey Strachan, who translated Andrei Makine, *Requiem for a Lost Empire,* from the French (New York: Simon and Schuster, 2001), 1.

31. See Harold D. Lasswell, "The Garrison State," in *American Journal of Sociology* 46, no. 4 (1941): 455–68. Given Lasswell's publication date, the piece is a prescient account of several dimensions of the Cold War and post–Cold War eras.

32. Thatcher's notorious remark has been quoted many times, often inaccurately. She made it during an interview with *Women's Own,* a British magazine, at No. 10 Downing Street on September 23, 1987. See *Women's Own,* October 31, 1987, 8–10. The interview transcript is also available at the Web site of the Margaret Thatcher Foundation, http://www.margaretthatcher.org/document/106689, accessed August 24, 2012.

33. Paul Kengor, *God and Ronald Reagan: A Spiritual Life* (New York: HarperCollins, 2004), 166. Kengor cites an interview conducted with Bob

Slosser at the Oval Office on October 14, 1983, for the Christian Broadcasting Network.

34. Cited in William Pfaff, *The Irony of Manifest Destiny: The Tragedy of American Foreign Policy* (New York: Walker, 2010), 73.

35. Dwight D. Eisenhower, "Remarks Recorded for the 'Back-to-God' Program of the American Legion," February 20, 1955, Posted online by Gerhard Peters and John T. Woolley for the American Presidency Project, http://www.presidency.ucsb.edu/ws/?pid=10414, accessed August 24, 2012. The program was broadcast nationally on radio and television.

36. See John Patrick Diggins, "Religion and the Founders," in *Partisan Review* 68, no. 3(2001): 371–78.

37. See Chas Freeman, "Nobody's Century," broadcast on *On Point with Tom Ashbrook*, October 22, 2012, http://onpoint.wbur.org/2012/10/22/nobodys-century, accessed December 10, 2012.

38. Dewey, *Quest for Certainty*, 9.

39. Ibid., 9.

40. Ted Hughes, "Echo and Narcissus," in *Tales from Ovid* (New York: Farrar, Straus and Giroux, 1997), 69–78.

41. Francis Fukuyama, *The End of History and the Last Man* (New York: Free Press, 1992).

42. Robert Jay Lifton and Greg Mitchell, *Hiroshima in America: A Half Century of Denial* (New York: Avon, 1996), xi.

43. Jill Ker Conway, *When Memory Speaks: Reflections on Autobiography* (New York: Knopf, 1998), chapter 1. See also my "What Memoir Forgets," *Nation*, July 27–August 3, 1998, 30–33.

44. André Malraux, *Anti-Memoirs*, trans. Terence Kilmartin (New York: Holt, Rinehart and Winston); see 1–8.

45. Van Wyck Brooks, "On Creating a Usable Past," *Dial*, April 11, 1918, 338–41.

46. Jean Baudrillard, *The Agony of Power* (Los Angeles: Semiotext(e), 2010), 72.

47. Bernard Lewis, *History: Remembered, Recovered, Invented* (Princeton: Princeton University Press, 1975); see especially "Masada and Cyrus," 3–42.

48. C. Vann Woodward, "The Irony of Southern History," in *The Burden of Southern History*, 3rd ed. (Baton Rouge: Louisiana State University Press, 1993), 187–211.

49. D. W. Brogan, "The Illusion of American Omnipotence," *Harper's*, December 1952, 21–28. See also "The Illusion of American Omnipotence—

Revisited," *Bulletin of the American Academy of Arts and Sciences* 20, no. 6 (1968): 2–10.

50. Reinhold Neibuhr, *The Irony of American History* (New York: Scribner, 1952), 18–19.

51. Woodward, "Irony of Southern History," 209–10.

Time and Time Again

1. Jean-Marie Colombani, "Nous sommes tous Américains," *Le Monde*, September 13, 2001, available on the newspaper's Web site, http://www .lemonde.fr/idees/article/2007/05/23/nous-sommes-tous-americains_913706 _3232.html, accessed August 24, 2012. The translation is mine.

2. "The War on Evil—President George W. Bush's Insights on Evil," November 13, 2001, The War on Evil Quotation Archive, http://irregulartimes .com/evilwar.html, accessed October 25, 2012.

3. See Frank Bruni, "For Bush, a Mission and a Defining Moment," *New York Times*, September 22, 2001.

4. Jean-Claude Maurice, *Si vous répétez, je d'émentirai* (Paris: Plon, 2009). William Pfaff provides an account of the occasion, as Chirac related it to Maurice, in *The Irony of American Destiny: The Tragedy of American Foreign Policy* (New York: Walker, 2010), 64–65. He translates the book's title as "If you repeat this, I'll deny it."

5. "Text of President Bush's Address Before a Joint Session of Congress," *New York Times*, September 21, 2001.

6. Condoleezza Rice, "Rethinking the National Interest: American Realism for a New World," *Foreign Affairs* 87, no. 4 (2008): 2–26. See also Pfaff, *Irony of American Destiny*, 91–93.

7. See Gustav Niebuhr, "Excerpts from Sermons Across the Nation," *New York Times*, September 17, 2001.

8. See Chancellor of the Exchequer Gordon Brown, text of a speech given to the Federal Reserve Bank, New York, November 16, 2001, http://www .hm-treasury.gov.uk/Newsroom_and_Speeches/Press/2001/press_126_01 .cfm. See George Soros, keynote address, the Asia Society Hong Kong Center, September 19, 2001. See also Lawrence Korb and Arnold Kohen, "A Marshall Plan for the Third World," *Boston Globe*, November 15, 2005, http:// www.boston.com/news/globe/editorial_opinion/oped/articles/2005/11/15/ a_marshall_plan_for_the_third_world/, accessed August 24, 2012.

9. George W. S. Trow, *Within the Context of No Context* (New York: Atlantic Monthly Press, 1997); see especially 43–45.

10. The Perle remark is cited frequently in the media, especially in Arab countries. See Jake Lynch, *Debates in Peace Journalism* (Sydney: Sydney University Press, 2008), 52.

11. See http://skycome.net/homelandSecurity/, accessed August 24, 2012.

12. See Michael Kammen, *Mystic Chords of Memory: The Transformation of Tradition in American Culture* (New York: Vintage, 1993), 271–77.

13. See Bernard DeVoto, *Across the Wide Missouri* (Boston: Houghton Mifflin, 1947). See also Margaret C. Conrads, ed., *Alfred Jacob Miller: Romancing the West* (Kansas City, Mo.: Nelson-Atkins Museum of Art, 2011).

14. "Golf, Gadgets and Gifts," *New York Times,* September 28, 2001.

15. "A Cliché, but Accurate," *New York Times,* October 9, 2001.

16. Bush's "Axis of Evil" speech is widely circulated. See American Rhetoric Online Speech Bank, http://www.americanrhetoric.com/speeches/stateoftheunion2002.htm or CNN.com, http://edition.cnn.com/2002/ALLPOLITICS/01/29/bush.speech.txt/, accessed August 24, 2012.

17. Ron Suskind, "Faith, Certainty and the Presidency of George Bush," *New York Times Sunday Magazine,* October 17, 2004. Rove was identified as "the aide" in Mark Danner, "Words in a Time of War: On Rhetoric, Truth and Power," in *What Orwell Didn't Know: Propaganda and the New Face of American Politics,* ed. András Szántó (New York: Public Affairs, 2007), 23.

18. Iraq Body Count, http://www.iraqbodycount.org/, accessed August 24, 2012. Costs of War, Eisenhower Study Group, Watson Institute for International Studies, Brown University, June 2011, http://costsofwar.org/article/afghan-civilians, accessed August 24, 2012. Note: Numerous projects have undertaken to monitor casualties in these two wars, and their figures vary widely. Those cited are conservative.

19. Daniel Halévy, *Essai sur l'Accélération de L'Histoire* (Paris: Les Isles d'Or, Éditions Self, 1948).

20. David Brion Davis, "The Enduring Legacy of the South's Civil War Victory," *New York Times,* August 26, 2001.

21. See the critique by Herbert Muschamp, "New War Memorial Is Shrine to Sentiment," *New York Times,* June 7, 2001.

22. Benjamin Barber, "A Revolution in Spirit," *Nation,* February 9, 2009, available athttp://www.thenation.com/article/revolution-spirit.

23. Dorothy Ross, "The Liberal Tradition Revisited and the Republican Tradition Addressed," in *New Directions in American Intellectual History,* ed. John Higham and Paul Keith Conklin (Baltimore: Johns Hopkins University Press, 1979), 116.

24. *Historia General de Guatemala* (Guatemala City: Asociación de Amigos del País, Fundación para la Cultura y Desarrollo, 1997). See also my "Memory Without History: Who Owns Guatemala's Past?" *Washington Quarterly* 24, no. 2 (2001): 59–72.

25. Woodrow Wilson, "Democracy and Efficiency," *Atlantic Monthly,* March 1901, 289–99.

26. See "Alexander Hamilton," *The American Experience,* Public Broadcasting System, Boston: WGBH, 2007, http://www.pbs.org/wgbh/amex/hamilton/, accessed October 30, 2011.

27. Henry Mackenzie published the novel *The Man of Feeling* in 1782. Cited in Andrew Burstein, *Sentimental Democracy: The Evolution of America's Self-Image* (New York: Hill and Wang, 1999); see especially xi–48 and 315–19. See also Walter Russell Mead, "The Jacksonian Tradition and American Foreign Policy," *National Interest,* Winter 1999–2000, 5–29.

28. Emmanuel Lévinas, *Time and the Other,* trans. Richard A. Cohen (Pittsburgh: Duquesne University Press, 1987); see especially 39–57.

29. Wendell L. Willkie, *One World* (New York: Simon and Schuster, 1943).

30. Carl L. Becker, *Progress and Power* (Stanford: Stanford University Press, 1936), 91. See also Robert S. Lynd, *Knowledge for What? The Place of Social Science in American Culture* (Princeton: Princeton University Press, 1939).

31. Paul Virilio, with Bertrand Richard, *The Administration of Fear,* trans. Ames Hodges (Los Angeles: Semiotext(e), 2012), 79.

32. Rice, "Rethinking the National Interest," 24.

33. Herbert Croly, *The Promise of American Life* (New York: Macmillan, 1909), 21.

34. Ibid., 17.

35. Ibid., 6.

36. Ibid., 22.

37. Ibid., 22–23.

38. Richard Rorty, *Achieving Our Country: Leftist Thought in Twentieth-Century America* (Cambridge: Harvard University Press, 1998); see "American National Pride: Whitman and Dewey," 3–38; the cited material appears on 11.

39. Croly, *Promise of American Life,* 18.

40. Jean Baudrillard, *The Agony of Power* (Los Angeles: Semiotext(e), 2010), 64.

41. "Is America Over? George Packer on Inequality and Social Decline; Joseph M. Parent and Paul K. MacDonald on the Need to Come Home," *Foreign Affairs* 90, no. 6 (2011); Packer's essay, "The Broken Contract," appears on 20–31, Parent and MacDonald's, "The Wisdom of Retrenchment," on 32–47. It is remarkable to note how clearly, after more than a century, we must still define our national conundrum as lying between empire abroad and democracy at home.

AN ACKNOWLEDGEMENT

—

Many people helped as this book developed, often without knowing they were making a contribution. There was talking and listening and arguing and correcting and (welcomely) an urging on. This was over a period of many years. I thank these people.

Certain among them I would like to mention. Carol Mann, my agent, was usefully insistent that I clarify my thoughts before setting out. Chris Rogers, my editor at Yale, brought a wonderful rigor to the task and a superior knowledge of the fields I was touching upon and the literature available to me as it pertained to many of them. My readers: What could I do without them? They were Sara Vagliano and Lloyd Garrison, to whom this book is dedicated; Lynn Dennison, my sister, and Peter Dimock, to whom special thanks for giving the benefit of his mind for history, for rhetoric and argument, and for writing. I also thank Godfrey Hodgson for his reading and comments once the project was drafted.

The library at the University Club in New York proved, once again, the unfailing fountainhead of all I.L.L.'s. Gratitude to Jane Reed and her colleagues.